College

THE MINISTRY OF LECTORS

Second Edition

James A. Wallace, C.Ss.R.

LITURGICAL PRESS
Collegeville, Minnesota

www.litpress.org

To the lectors at Holy Trinity Parish,
Georgetown, Washington, D.C.
in gratitude for their service
to the People of God

Design by Joachim Rhoades, O.S.B.
Cover image by Gene Plaisted, O.S.C.

The author is grateful for quotations from the following liturgical texts:
Lectionary for *Mass for use in the Dioceses of the United States of America,*
second typical edition, copyright © 1998, 1997, 1970 by the Confrater-
nity of Christian Doctrine, Washington, D.C. All rights reserved.

The English translation of the Introduction to the *Lectionary for Mass* ©
1981, International Committee on English in the Liturgy, Inc. All rights
reserved. Altered by the National Conference of Catholic Bishops.

The English translation of the *Book of Blessings* © 1987, International
Committee on English in the Liturgy, Inc. All rights reserved.

1	2	3	4	5	6	7	8

Library of Congress Cataloging-in-Publication Data

Wallace, James A., 1944–
    The ministry of lectors / James A. Wallace. — 2nd ed.
      p. cm. — (Collegeville ministry series)
    Includes bibliographical references.
    ISBN 0-8146-2953-9 (pbk. : alk. paper)
    1. Lay readers. I. Title. II. Series.
  BV677.W35   2004
  264'.34—dc22   2003025634

Contents

Introduction

The novelist Anna Quindlen has said that people read to know they are not alone. Reading brings us into worlds real and imaginary, introduces us to people wise and foolish, and provides us with knowledge and insight. Reading brings to us other voices with different perspectives. The American novelist Eudora Welty wrote that from the time she was a child and was introduced to the world of books, she knew that, whether her mother read to her or she was reading to herself, the voice she heard was not her voice or her mother's but the voice of the text. This is a wonderful insight. A text has a voice—sometimes more than one—that speaks to us and, when we read to others, it speaks through us. A good book begins as the dark markings of print on a page but ends as a companion with whom we have spent hours and whose voice might well have an enduring impact on our lives. Then, too, there are those great books, or passages in a book, that we return to again and again, to savor, learn from, delight in, or lean against for comfort and consolation in times of distress and sorrow.

Such a book is the Bible. It is really a collection of books, some of which have been around close to three thousand years. It brings us stories of beginnings and visions of endings, sagas of ancestral lineage, and tales of royal families whose men and women listened for the voice of God over the call of their own desires. Within its pages are snippets of wisdom in couplet form and prophetic utterances in poetic meter, letters of instruction and advice and homilies of theological depth and emotional appeal, prayers of longing and lament, and songs of praise and exaltation.

From the pages of the Bible, selections have been made for the worship life of many Christian communities of faith and put into a book called the Lectionary. There are a number of such lectionaries at present. In the United States the two principal ones are the *Lectionary for Mass* used by Roman Catholics and the *Revised Common Lectionary* used by many churches in the Protestant tradition. Whenever these communities gather, whether on Sundays or to celebrate other special acts of worship and praise, men and women educated to the task are called upon to read the sacred texts. The name given to those who perform this work is "lector," a word rooted in the Latin word *legere*, which means "to read."

This book for lectors is divided into three parts. The first part considers three different ways of understanding the role of the lector: as a job, a ministry, and a vocation. The second section will then reflect on the mystery of the word of God. Our God speaks *to* us in the Scriptures. Whether a community reads from a Bible or from a Lectionary, the word of the Lord comes once more to dwell in our midst, to take up residence in our hearts and minds, so that it might bear fruit in our lives. God continues to speak to us through human words. As in the past, God calls men and women in our own day to help bring this divine self-revelation about. The third part will then focus on how we can cooperate in bringing to fulfillment God's decision to speak not only to but also *through* us. Here we get down to practical matters by looking at the two areas of spiritual preparation and speaking preparation. The former will suggest a process for opening one's mind and heart to the word, while the latter will consider the requirements for a satisfying public reading that are located in the needs of the text, the listeners, and the liturgical setting. Three suggestions for ongoing development as a lector will conclude this section.

Both spirit and flesh are involved in the preparation to lector. The spirit of the lector is called to surrender to the Spirit of the Lord who truly gives us words to speak. The Holy Spirit is at the heart of the word's bearing fruit: "The working of the Holy Spirit is needed if the Word of God is to make what we hear outwardly have its effect inwardly. . . . The working of the

Holy Spirit precedes, accompanies, and brings to completion the whole celebration of the Liturgy" (Introduction to the *Lectionary for Mass*, 9). As it was from the beginning, the Holy Spirit continues to come upon those called to serve and to work through their very being. Thus, the body of the lector—which includes the entire person: mind, imagination, and feelings, as well as facial expression and muscular response—is invited to submit to the body of the text and to embody its thoughts and feelings as faithfully and fully as possible.

I am grateful to the many lectors with whom I have worked and celebrated the liturgy over the last thirty-three years, particularly the lectors who serve so well the people of Holy Trinity Parish, Georgetown, in Washington, D.C. Their love of the Word of God has been an inspiration; their passionate proclamation of it has led to its being heard in ever new and fruitful ways. May the word they have sown so well in the lives of others continue to bear a rich harvest in their own. A special word of thanks to my colleagues and friends who were kind enough to read this work and offer suggestions: Margaret Costello, Judith Gilbert, Mary Johnston, Patrick Towell, and, most especially, Daniel Grigassy, O.F.M.

James A. Wallace, C.Ss.R.
August 1, 2003—Feast of St. Alphonsus de Liguori

PART ONE

The Lector—What's in a Name?

This work has been written for all who read the biblical texts during the Liturgy of the Word, including those who proclaim the gospel. It is offered to those who have been doing it for a while, those who are about to begin, and even those who might be considering such a commitment to the liturgical life of the community and want to know what it involves. As with so many of the things we do in life, there are different ways we might think about and approach the role of the lector in the liturgy. Three such ways, not meant to be mutually exclusive, will now be considered:

1. *A Job*

You might react to the word *job* as being too pedestrian, too mundane, not worthy of this liturgical office, even possibly undermining the reverence that should inform our attitude to this important task. But I would propose that it is not being disrespectful to recognize that the public reading of the Scriptures is *work*; it is an important *job* that needs to be done with competence and skill in order that the worship of the community can take place. Liturgy literally means the *work* of the people—from the Greek *leitos* (people) and *ergon* (work). Within that context of a community of faith gathering to do its most important work—the celebration of the Eucharist as an act of praise to God through Jesus in the power of the Holy Spirit—reading the Scriptures is a labor of love. It requires having both knowledge and certain skills for the work to be done in a manner satisfying to all. So, as a starting point, I invite you to think of the office of lector as a job. And, as they say, "Somebody's got to do it." Unless the Liturgy of the Word is done well, the foundation will not be laid for what follows in the Liturgy of the Sacrament.

The reform of the Roman Catholic liturgy, most notably the Liturgy of the Eucharist, brought out the different tasks involved when the community gathers for liturgy. Certain distinct roles need to be filled: presider, deacon, acolyte, lector, cantor, choir, usher, and eucharistic minister. The work of the lector involves reading the biblical texts during the Liturgy of the Word. To be an effective lector calls for adequate preparation that includes study, prayer, and practice. A lector is given the task of approaching with reverence that complex body of sacred literature we call the Scriptures, once described by no less a light than St. Augustine as "of mountainous difficulty and enveloped in mysteries." Furthermore, while anyone might be able to read, I would suggest that not all who can read are able to lector—at least not right away. You only have to go to a liturgy when someone is plucked out of the congregation to realize that, or to a wedding or funeral when a member of the family has been chosen to read simply because he or she is a member of the family, often resulting in a halting, hard to hear, rushed reading.

These last statements are not meant to be elitist. St. Isidore of Seville, a doctor of the Church, wrote that a lector should be "deeply versed in doctrine and books and thoroughly adorned with the knowledge and meaning of words" so that the reading "would move the minds and feelings" of the listeners. Unless the readings are done well, people will not hear God's voice speaking through these texts and be truly nourished at the table of the word. So the work of the lector is essential, and it cannot be assumed that all have this talent. "There are different kinds of spiritual gifts. . . ," as Paul reminded the Corinthians (1 Cor 12:4). We might add to the gifts Paul names in that letter those important for the worship of the community: presiding, preaching, serving, singing, and, especially, considering its place at the outset of every liturgy, proclaiming the Scriptures. All these are gifts given for the sake of the body, the Church, which brings us to the second understanding of the lector's task.

2. *A Ministry*

The office of lector is also a ministry. The word *ministry*, also from the Latin, means to serve, and offers another perspective on the role of the lector: a form of service to the community. The *General Instruction of the Roman Missal* observes: "By tradition, the function of proclaiming the readings is ministerial, not presidential. The readings, therefore, should be proclaimed by a lector . . ." (59).[1] What this means is that the role of the lector does not belong to the presider but to others who have been called to serve in this particular way. The ministries of reader and acolyte were restored by Pope Paul VI in the apostolic letter *Ministeria quaedam* in 1972. In this letter Pope Paul wrote that these ministries "may be committed to lay Christians; hence they are no longer reserved to candidates for the sacrament of orders" (6). The Introduction to the *Lectionary for Mass* (hereafter, LMIn) comments on the importance of this ministry: "In the hearing of God's word the Church is built up and grows . . ." (7). The readings within the liturgy serve to nourish and sustain the body of Christ. In the formal rite of institution of readers, the bishop gives the Bible to each candidate and says: "Take this book of Scripture and be faithful in handing on the word of God, so that it may grow strong in the hearts of his people."

While the rite of institution is reserved to men, it can be helpful for all lectors to meditate on the words suggested for the conclusion of the bishop's homily on this occasion:

> . . . through his Son, who became man for us, God the Father has revealed the mystery of salvation and brought it to fulfillment. Jesus Christ made all things known to us and then entrusted his Church with the mission of preaching the Gospel to the whole world.
>
> As readers and bearers of God's word, you will assist in this mission, and so take on a special office within the Christian community; you will be given a responsibility in the service of the faith, which is rooted in the word of God. You will proclaim that word in the liturgical assembly. . . . Thus with your help men and women will come to know God our Father and his Son Jesus Christ, whom he sent, and so be able to reach eternal life.

The ministry of lector continues the mission of preaching the word by proclaiming it in the liturgical assembly. Lectors do this "in the service of the faith." The words Paul wrote to the Romans about the importance of preaching can also be heard to apply to lectors: "How shall they call on the Lord in whom they have not believed? And how shall they believe unless they have heard of him? And how shall they hear unless there is someone to preach? . . . Faith, then, comes through hearing and what is heard is the word of Christ" (Rom 10:14, 17).

The third edition of the *General Instruction of the Roman Missal* outlines the following as the duties of this ministry:

Introductory Rites

194. In coming to the altar, when no deacon is present, the lector, wearing approved attire, may carry the *Book of the Gospels*, which is to be slightly elevated. In that case, the lector walks in front of the priest but otherwise along with the other ministers.

195. Upon reaching the altar, the lector makes a profound bow with the others. If he (sic) is carrying the *Book of the Gospels*, he (sic) approaches the altar and places the *Book of the Gospels* upon it. Then the lector takes his (sic) own place in the sanctuary with the other ministers.

The Liturgy of the Word

196. The lector reads from the ambo the readings that precede the Gospel. If there is no psalmist, the lector may also proclaim the responsorial Psalm after the first reading.

197. When no deacon is present, the lector, after the introduction by the priest, may announce from the ambo the intentions of the Prayer of the Faithful.

198. If there is no singing at the Entrance or at Communion and the antiphons in the Missal are not recited by the faithful, the lector may read them at the appropriate time.

3. *A Vocation*

The universal call to holiness and to witness to Christ in the world comes to fulfillment differently in each of us. One expression of this universal call can be found in the ministry of reader. While baptism and confirmation in the Spirit have made all of Christ's faithful into messengers of God's word and all are to be bearers of that word both in the Church and in the world, at least by the witness of their lives, lectors carry out this task in a unique way by entering into an intimate relationship with the sacred texts so central to the worship life of the community. They are called to a deep relationship with God specifically through the words of Scripture, this treasured legacy that has been preserved and handed down for thousands of years. Drawing closer to our God who speaks through the Scriptures is an invitation this ministry offers to you. Listen again to the rite of institution and its concluding words:

> In proclaiming God's word to others, accept it yourselves in obedience to the Holy Spirit. Meditate on it constantly, so that each day you will have a deeper love of the Scriptures, and in all you say and do show forth to the world our Savior, Jesus Christ.

As God called to Moses from the burning bush, so God calls to you from the sacred book: "Come, draw closer. Meet me in my word." As God called to Mary to enflesh the divine word, so God calls every lector to allow once again the Word to become flesh, *your* flesh. God waits on your response: "Let it be done to me according to your word."

KEEP IN MIND

- To be an effective lector calls for adequate preparation that includes study, prayer, and practice.
- Unless the readings are done well, people will not hear God's voice speaking through these texts and be truly nourished at the table of the word.
- The ministry of lector continues the mission of preaching the Word by proclaiming it in the liturgical assembly.
- Lectors are called to a deep relationship with God specifically through the words of Scripture, this treasured legacy that has been preserved and handed down for thousands of years.

PART TWO

God's Word Spoken to Us

At the end of every reading, the lector says, "The word of the Lord," and the people respond, "Thanks be to God." These two phrases easily become routine. But take a moment and think about what you are saying to the people when you state this five-word proclamation: "The word of the Lord." We believe that when we read these fragments of ancient texts selected from the Bible for the liturgy, "God speaks to his people, Christ is still proclaiming the Gospel" (Constitution on the Sacred Liturgy, 33).[2] God has chosen to use human language as a way to communicate with us.

The first thing to keep in mind is that words are human creations with many of the qualities characteristic of human beings, including the potential to bring life and joy, ambiguity and confusion, even profound sorrow and death. Like their human makers, words can be misunderstood and misinterpreted as well as console and comfort. The poet Ann Sexton once wrote that words are both "daisies and bruises."[3] They can fall upon the mind and heart like water upon the parched earth or they can penetrate the spirit like "a two-edged sword, piercing so deeply that it divides soul and spirit, joints and marrow" (Heb 4:12). How they are used and what they achieve is up to those who wield them. We know the power of such simple words as "I love you" and "You can count on me" as well as the weight of such succinct phrases as "It's over" and "She's gone." At their best, words take root and empower us as individuals and as a community to move toward each other in love, justice, and peace and toward God in faith, hope, and unwavering confidence.

Words are the basic building blocks of both communication and community, both of which have to do with communion, coming together in unity. When we communicate with another, we strive to enter into a meeting of minds and hearts. It does not mean there will be immediate communion with the other, but, ultimately, that is the goal of all communication. Sometimes communication only takes us to a state of mutual understanding; we know what the other is saying, although we do not agree with it. But the ancient discipline of rhetoric had as its goal to persuade those listening, to bring listeners to a common understanding and to a common purpose, to form a community of shared attitudes, values, and actions dedicated to the common good.

The playwright Tom Stoppard in his play *The Real Thing*[4] has one of his characters say that while writers may not be sacred, *words are*. And so words deserve respect because if you bring the right ones together, you might move the world a little closer to peace or even create a poem that children will remember after you are gone. The words of Scripture are sacred words to those who believe; they can even evoke faith in those who do not believe. St. Paul writes that "faith comes from what is heard, and what is heard comes through the word of Christ" (Rom 10:17). And the mission of Christ, the word of God, was summed up on the night before he died, when Jesus prayed: ". . . not only for them but also for those who will believe in me through their word, so that they may all be one, as you, Father, are in me and I am in you, so also may they be one in us, that the world may believe that you sent me" (John 17:21).

The word of God has a particular meaning in the Roman Catholic tradition. Vatican II's Constitution on Divine Revelation states: "Tradition and scripture make up a single sacred deposit of the word of God, which is entrusted to the church" (10). For believers baptized into the Roman Catholic Church, the word of God embraces Sacred Scripture as "the utterance of God put down as it is in writing under the inspiration of the Holy Spirit" (9) and the tradition which has been handed on orally in the preaching and teaching of the Church. "Thus God, who spoke in the past, continues to converse with the spouse of his beloved Son. And the Holy Spirit, through whom the living voice of the Gospel rings out in the church—and through it in the world—leads believers to the full truth and makes the word of Christ dwell in them in all its richness" (see Col 3:16) (8). It is the word of God found in Scripture that is our particular concern here.

The Word of God and the Bible

The Bible witnesses to the power and the purpose of the word of God. The power of God's word is revealed both in creation and redemption. In the opening words of the Bible we have a testimony to the power of the word at creation when the author of Genesis writes: "Then God said, 'Let there be light,' and there was light" (Gen 1:3). Again and again in the opening chapter we hear "Then God said . . ." followed by "And so it happened." The power of God's word reveals itself first as a creative word, calling forth the richness of our world from a formless wasteland. God's word is revealed as one that shapes and designs, contains and expands, divides and diversifies. It is this creative word that also calls forth a people. "Who created you, O Jacob, and formed you, O Israel?" (Isa 43:1a), God asks, and then goes on to remind the people of God's power to redeem:

> Fear not, for I have redeemed you;
>> I have called you by name; you are mine.
> When you pass through the water, I will be with you;
>> in the rivers you shall not drown.
> When you walk through fire, you shall not be burned;
>> the flames shall not consume you.
> For I am the Lord, your God,
>> the Holy One of Israel, your savior. (Isa 43:1b-3a)

But while God's word is active and initiates, going forth with a purpose, it also expects a response:

> For just as from the heavens
>> the rain and snow come down

> And do not return there
>> till they have watered the earth,
>> making it fertile and fruitful,
> Giving seed to him who sows
>> and bread to him who eats,
> So shall my word be
>> that goes forth from my mouth;
> It shall not return to me void,
>> but shall do my will,
>> achieving the end for which I sent it. (Isa 55:10-11)

In all of this we find reflected the Hebrew understanding of the word as an event. When God speaks, something happens: creation, redemption, sanctification. God's word is an effective word, bringing about the fulfillment of what it promises.

In the New Testament, we know that "Jesus came to Galilee proclaiming the gospel of God: 'This is the time of fulfillment. The kingdom of God is at hand. Repent and believe in the Gospel'" (Mark 1:14-15). He spoke in parables about the power of the word in the imagery of a sower going out to sow seeds, and while not all the seed landed on good earth, what did reaped a rich harvest. He spoke in images of mustard seeds and lost sheep, of rebellious sons and women who did not bring enough oil for their lamps, of kings who calculated what was needed for battle and widows who badgered judges for justice. By the time the Fourth Gospel was written, Jesus himself was recognized as the word who "became flesh and made his dwelling among us" (John 1: 14) and as the one who said, "The words I have spoken to you are spirit and life" (John 6:63).

The Bible itself witnesses to the fact that the word of God (the Scriptures) assists in understanding *the* word of God (Jesus). When the risen Lord appears to the disciples on the road to Emmaus, he turns to the Scriptures to help them understand: "Then beginning with Moses and all the prophets, he interpreted to them what referred to him in all the scriptures" (Luke 24:27). And, similar to the Isaiah text that speaks of the fruitfulness of the word, Jesus in the great discourse in the Gospel of John on the night before he died (John 13:31–17:26), after saying to his disciples that he is the vine, they the branches, and his Father the vine grower who prunes so that the branches will bear fruit, then goes on to say, "You are already pruned because of the word that I spoke to you" (John 15:3).

In the First Letter to Timothy we hear about the ongoing usefulness of the word of God: "All Scripture is inspired by God and is useful for teaching, for refutation, for correction, and for training for righteousness, so that one who belongs to God may be competent, equipped for every good work" (1 Tim 3:16-17). Thus, the Bible offers us a dynamic portrait of God's word in various activities: creating, redeeming, instructing, correcting, encouraging, sanctifying, and shaping a people of faith, hope, and love. Is it any wonder that when it came time to reform the liturgy at the Second Vatican Council the importance of Scripture came to the fore?

The Word of God and the Liturgy

The reading of the Scriptures during community worship has its roots in the Jewish synagogue service where the first reading was from the Torah, that is, the first five books of the Bible, followed by a reading from one of the Prophets, which served to comment on the Torah selection. In Luke 4:16, we have Jesus going into the synagogue at Nazareth on the Sabbath, taking up the scroll, and reading from the text of Isaiah 61:1 "The spirit of the Lord is upon me, for he has anointed me to bring good news to the poor. . . ." The Christian community kept this tradition of reading from the Sacred Scripture when it gathered to celebrate the Eucharist. In the earliest description of what took place on Sunday, St. Justin Martyr wrote in the mid-second century a description of the service: "On the day which is called Sunday we have a common assembly of all who live in the cities or in the outlying districts, and the memoirs of the Apostles or the writings of the prophets are read, as long as there is time. . . ."[5] He goes on to describe the rest of the service, including preaching, prayers of the faithful, the presentation of bread and wine, a prayer of thanksgiving, and reception of the eucharistic elements. From the beginning, the word of God was part of the community's worship.

As a boy growing up in the 1950s, I can remember being told that in order to satisfy the obligation of Sunday Mass you had to be in the church by the reading of the gospel. (Others remember the "deadline" being the taking of the veil from the chalice at what was then called the Offertory of the Mass.) At that time Catholics were only beginning to be encouraged to read the Bible, or at least to have a missal to read the English translation of the readings during the Mass, while the priest read them in Latin. But "going to Mass" was then equated with being present for "the principal parts of the Mass": the Offertory, the Consecration, and Communion. It was not until the Constitution on the Sacred Liturgy, promulgated in 1963, that we returned to an understanding of the Mass as composed of the Liturgy of the Word and the Liturgy of the Eucharist, two parts forming one holy action.

The Constitution proclaims the many ways in which Christ is present during liturgical celebrations: "He is present in the sacrifice of the Mass both in the person of his minister . . . and most of all in the eucharistic species. . . . He is present in his word since it is he himself who speaks when the holy scriptures are read in church. Lastly he is present when the church prays and sings, for he has promised 'where two or three are gathered together in my name there am I in the midst of them'" (7). The *General Instruction of the Roman Missal* expanded on this recognition of the presence of Christ in the word, noting that "in the readings, explained by the homily, God is speaking to his people, opening up to them the mystery of redemption and salvation, and nourishing their spirit; Christ is present to the faithful through his own word" (33).

The image of the word as a form of nourishment is especially pertinent, for it invited Roman Catholics to recognize the centrality of the table of the word as equal to the table of the Eucharist: "The Church is nourished spiritually at the table of God's word and at the table of the Eucharist: from the one it grows in wisdom and from the other in holiness. In the word of God the divine covenant is announced; in the Eucharist, the new and everlasting covenant is renewed. The spoken word of God brings to mind the history of salvation; the Eucharist embodies it in the sacramental signs of the liturgy" (LMIn, 10).

The re-cognition, that is, the "knowing-again" of the presence of Christ in the word, led to the decision to offer the community of faith a greater exposure to the Bible. The Constitution on the Sacred Liturgy declared: "The treasures of the Bible are to be opened up more lavishly so that a richer fare may be provided for the faithful at the table of God's word. In this way a more significant part of the sacred scriptures will be read to the people over a fixed number of years" (51). The result of this declaration was the *Lectionary for Mass* with its expanded offering of texts for both the Sunday, weekday, and special occasion liturgical celebrations.

The Word of God and the Lectionary

A lectionary has been defined as "a book or list of readings of scripture for the church year."[6] The Lectionary is not the same thing as the Bible. As Andrew D. Ciferni so cogently expressed, lectionaries "are creations of the churches. The Scriptures are inspired; lectionaries are not."[7] Lectionaries go back to the fifth and sixth centuries. The earliest forms contained ordered listings of selections that would be proclaimed on Sundays and feasts. Martin Connell writes that during this time when all texts were hand-written, "there was usually one sacred book for each worshiping community, and in the margins of that book were markers saying things like 'Start here' or 'Stop here.'"[8] Lectionaries organized more systematically according to the liturgical year and with full readings began to appear in the thirteenth century. But it was the Council of Trent (1545–1563) that provided the Lectionary that determined most Catholics' exposure to Scripture for almost four centuries. The readings selected for the Missal of Pius V help us appreciate all the more the richness and variety we now have in the revised Lectionary of 1969.

The Missal of Pius V had a one-year Sunday lectionary cycle. Each year the same 120 passages from Scripture would be heard on Sundays and holy days of obligation. Of the forty-six books of the Old Testament, selections came from only ten of them, but not one Old Testament reading was assigned to Sundays. Most Catholics, then, had little, if any, exposure to the Old

Testament, which provides the foundation for any understanding of the New Testament. From the New Testament, seventeen of the twenty-seven books provided readings, but nothing from the book of Revelation or eight of the shorter letters. As for the Gospels, all four were represented, but the most readings came from Matthew (24) and Luke (21), followed by John (17), and then Mark (4).[9] The result is that Catholics would hear during the year about 17 percent of the New Testament and—if one attended Mass on Epiphany, Ash Wednesday, Good Friday, and Easter Vigil, about 1 percent of the Old Testament. As for weekdays, either the two readings from the previous Sunday—one from the letters of the New Testament and one from the Gospels—were repeated at daily Masses, or a Requiem Mass was celebrated with its own readings, except during Lent and certain feasts of the saints, which had their own readings.

The 1969 revised *Lectionary for Mass,* then, was one of the major liturgical accomplishments of Vatican II. It offered a far more expansive selection from both the Old and New Testaments, providing that "richer fare" at the table of the word that the Constitution on the Sacred Liturgy called for. A three-year Sunday and festive cycle offers three readings: the first from the Old Testament (except during the Easter season when Acts of the Apostles is read); a second reading from an apostle (either from a Letter or from the book of Revelation, depending on the season), and the third reading from one of the Gospels (Matthew, Mark, and Luke each having a year in the Sunday cycle during Ordinary Time with John featured during the liturgical seasons, especially Lent and Easter, and for several weeks during the Sunday B cycle). In the course of the three-year Sunday cycle, every New Testament book is given some exposure, except for 2 and 3 John and Jude, which do show up in the weekday readings. The major feasts of the Lord, of Mary, and of certain saints—Peter and Paul, John the Baptist—also have special readings.

The recently revised edition of the *Lectionary for Mass* (Second Typical Edition, 1997) in four volumes offers further refinements, additional texts, and a new layout, although with little substantial change in the selections. The four volumes are divided in the following way:

- Volume I: Sundays (Cycles A, B, C), Solemnities, Feasts of the Lord and the Saints;
- Volume II: Proper of Seasons for Weekdays: Year I, Proper of the Saints, Common of the Saints;
- Volume III: Proper of Seasons for Weekdays: Year II, Proper of the Saints, Common of the Saints;
- Volume IV: Common of Saints, Ritual Masses, Masses for Various Needs and Occasions, Votive Masses, and Masses for the Dead.

Lectors will usually be involved with the first three volumes dealing with Sunday (vol. I) and weekday celebrations of the liturgy (vols. II and III). However, it is good to be aware of the fourth volume and how it is arranged.

Since 1993 there has also been a *Lectionary for Masses with Children,* (hereafter LMC), intended "as a means of enabling children to participate in liturgical celebrations."[10] This Lectionary contains simplified language and carefully chosen Scripture passages and its goal is to enable children to celebrate *their* faith in relation to their age and developmental level and to gradually lead children into the worship of the adult Christian community. The Introduction to the LMC notes that it adheres as closely as possible to the selection and arrangement of readings found in the *Lectionary for Mass,* while adapting them to the needs of children (11). Furthermore, keeping in mind the entire assembly, the Introduction clearly states that the LCM "should not be used exclusively or even preferentially at Sunday Masses, even though large numbers of children are present" (13).

Two principles govern the Order of Readings for Sundays and festive days; they are called the principles of "harmony" and of "semi-continuous reading." The principle of harmony comes into play during Ordinary Time in the choice of the first reading to correlate with or in some way prefigure the gospel of the day. There is harmony of another kind between all three readings chosen during Advent and Christmas, Lent and Easter, according to the character of each season: Advent with its themes of the first and second comings of the Lord; Christmas with its focus on the mystery of the Incarnation; Lent with its emphasis on Christian initiation, repentance, conversion, and the history of salvation; and Easter with its recounting of the various appearances of the risen Lord, the early church's witness and growth, and living out of Easter faith in today's world. The principle of "semi-continuous reading" governs the gospels and second readings of the Sundays of Ordinary Time, during which a book will be read straight through, though not every chapter and verse.

The structure of the Sunday Liturgy of the Word includes the first reading, the responsorial psalm, the second reading, an alleluia with verse, and the gospel. There is a deliberate pacing called for in the Liturgy of the Word to benefit its being heard by the community: listening, silence, response (responsorial psalm), listening, silence, preparation for the gospel (alleluia), listening to the gospel, preaching, silence, prayer of the faithful. Ideally there is an interplay between proclamation and silence, spoken word and sung response. The Liturgy of the Word can be truly seen as a concelebrated liturgy with parts played by priest (the homily), deacon (the gospel), lectors (first and second readings), cantor (responsorial psalm), and the community who listens, reflects, responds, and sings. Furthermore, the integrity of the Liturgy of the Word and the Liturgy of the Eucharist can be seen in how the community moves from hearing the word of God in Scripture and the homily, thereby coming to recognize God's ongoing and active presence in our lives, to giving thanks for that gracious presence in the prayer of Eucharist, and then partaking in Holy Communion with the Lord and one another.

The two-year Weekday Cycle during Ordinary Time provides a semi-continuous reading of two texts, with a two-year cycle for the first reading and a one-year cycle for the gospels. The seasons of Advent and Christmas, Lent and Easter have their own one-year cycle of weekday readings. Provision is also made for readings for the celebration of the saints recognized in the universal calendar, and also for Masses for special occasions and intentions, and the liturgical celebrations of the other sacraments.

What holds the readings together in all seasons is what God has done for us in Christ, most notably in the saving mysteries of the Incarnation and the Paschal Mystery of Christ's dying and rising. While more can be said about the Lectionary, a final word of advice would be to take time to become familiar with how it is set up. Start with the *Lectionary for Mass* for Sundays (vol. I). A further suggestion would be to read the Introduction to the Lectionary, found in all four volumes, to understand more fully the vision and principles on which it is based.

The Word of God and the Lector

The word of God as found in the Bible and organized in the Lectionary serves the prayer life of the Christian community in the course of the liturgical year. This word comes to the lector in the form of print on the page. While we say in faith, "The word of the Lord" or "The Gospel of the Lord" after every reading, the act of reading also remains an event of human communication. Between the text and the community stands the lector. Whether one approaches reading as a job, a ministry, a vocation, or all three, there is a need for human engagement on the part of the lector with the texts. "In the beginning was the Word," the Gospel of John declares in its magnificent prologue (1:1). And that remains true every Sunday. In the beginning of the worship service is the word, waiting to be spoken and heard. It waits to become flesh—first, the flesh of the lector, then the flesh of the community. It needs to be embodied to be a living word, embodied in speech and action. And that leads us to the ministry of the lector.

Scripture must be communicated as a word of life, a weighty word that allows God to reach out and touch our hearts, to make contact with our souls, to transform us into the full stature of our status as children of God. For this to happen, lectors must prepare. And this preparation is twofold: spiritual and technical. The word of God *to* us will only reach its destination if it becomes the word of God *through* us. One instrument that God has chosen to communicate through when the people of God gather for worship is the lector. Let us now consider some of the steps that help us to fulfill God's plan.

KEEP IN MIND

- Words are the basic building blocks of both communication and community, both of which have to do with communion, coming together in unity.

- "Tradition and scripture make up a single sacred deposit of the word of God, which is entrusted to the church."

- The Bible offers us a dynamic portrait of God's word in various activities: creating, redeeming, instructing, correcting, encouraging, sanctifying, and shaping a people of faith, hope, and love.

- "The Church is nourished spiritually at the table of God's word and at the table of the Eucharist: from the one it grows in wisdom and from the other in holiness."

- A deliberate pacing is called for in the Liturgy of the word to assure that the community hears the word of God: listening, silence, response (responsorial psalm), listening, silence, preparation for the gospel (alleluia), listening, preaching, silence, prayer of the faithful. Silence is frequently neglected.

- God's word waits to become flesh—first, the flesh of the lector, then the flesh of the community.

PART THREE

God's Word Spoken Through Us

When you think of preparing to lector, it may seem the main task is to practice the readings aloud. But preparing to lector involves not only speech preparation but also spiritual preparation. Years ago I remember reading Mortimer Adler's *How to Read a Book*, and I have never forgotten his wry definition of a lecture as the process whereby the notes of the teacher become the notes of the student without passing through the head of either. Something similar can happen not only when preparing to read the Scriptures but in the actual moment of proclaiming the word. The print on the page can be translated into sound coming from your mouth, but the reading has not passed through your head, heart, or soul. To avoid this happening, the first stage of preparing to lector is to engage in some kind of spiritual preparation. Here are some suggestions.

Spiritual Preparation

Step One: Pray. You are approaching holy ground as much as Moses did when he heard the voice calling out to him from the burning bush (Exod 3:4ff.). Moses was told to take off his sandals because he was approaching a place where God was present. So, too, is the lector who goes to the ambo to proclaim the word of God. But reverence for the word is not to be confined to the moment of proclamation. It begins in the preparation. When you first open to the readings—and the earlier the better—say a prayer as simple as: "Come, Holy Spirit, help me to hear the word of God, to understand this word, and to proclaim it with faith to your people."

Step Two: Listen to the Word. For the word of God to be given expression through us, we have to allow it to make an impression on us. Before speaking the word of God to others, you have to hear it yourself—a deep down hearing. There needs to be time for the word to seep into the head and heart of anyone who hopes to bring God's word to the community. The first step is listening, but listening is not easy. An article in the *Washington Post*[11] some time ago noted the importance and difficulty of this profoundly human act, using statistics from the International Listening Association. First of all, about 85 percent of what we know we have learned by listening, and we spend 45 percent of our time listening. However, we are distracted, preoccupied, or forgetful about 75 percent of the time; and immediately after listening to someone, we usually remember only about half of what we have heard, and after a short time that drops to 20 percent. So, one conclusion is while we may hear a great deal, we are not very skilled at listening.

Yet we know that if any relationship is going to get beyond a superficial stage or get through a troubled one, listening to the other person plays a crucial role. This is also true when it comes to our relationship with God. We need to spend time listening to God's word, straining at times to hear what God is trying to say to us here and now, both in the events of our lives, in the silence of our prayer, and in the word of God entrusted to us in the Scriptures and the living tradition of the Church. So let us begin with an exercise in listening. Take a moment and read this text assigned as the second reading on Pentecost Sunday (12:3b-7, 12-13):

A Reading from the First Letter of Saint Paul to the Corinthians

Brothers and sisters:

No one can say, "Jesus is Lord," except by the Holy Spirit.
There are different kinds of spiritual gifts but the same Spirit;
  there are different forms of service but the same Lord;

> there are different workings but the same God
> who produces all of them in everyone.
> To each individual the manifestation of the Spirit
> is given for some benefit.
>
> As a body is one though it has many parts,
> and all the parts of the body, though many, are one body,
> so also Christ.
> For in one Spirit we were all baptized into one body,
> whether Jews or Greeks, slaves or free persons,
> and we were all given to drink of one Spirit.
>
> The word of the Lord.

Now, most likely you just read this to yourself, that is, silently, hearing it in your mind, as you were taking it in through your eyes. That is the way most of us have been reading since we were in school and we were told to take out our book and read *in silence*. But this was not always the usual way of reading. In the *Confessions of St. Augustine*, book Six, the saint talks about being surprised when he entered the study of Bishop Ambrose of Milan and found the great preacher and teacher reading to himself.[12] It was the custom at that time to read aloud. And that is what I would ask you to do now. Go back to that text and read it again but this time out loud.

What is the difference between reading something to yourself and reading it aloud? More effort is required, certainly. Also, reading out loud slows you down. But something else can also begin to happen. You may find yourself giving emphasis to certain words as distinct from others. You may find you are pausing, coloring some words with a particular emotional tone. You start to enter more deeply into an understanding of the thought the words convey and perhaps even more so into the feelings that run under the words.

Now, listen once more, only this time, cup your hands over your ears and speak the words aloud. You will find you do not have to do it loudly at all. Speak them to yourself. But listen to them with full attention, as if for the first time. Read them slowly—thoughtfully, with feeling, pondering their meaning. If you find your attention drifts for a moment, go back and read the phrase again. If you find that a particular phrase speaks to you, repeat it. The goal is not to get to the end of the reading as quickly as possible but to allow the reading to enter your being. Savor the words. Taste them. Chew them. (Do it now.)

What was this experience like for you? What did you hear? Was there something you heard this time that did not come through in the first two readings? Did you discover the voice of the text by this way of listening? It comes as a more interior voice, a voice coming from within. I have done this exercise with preachers, asking them to give their full attention to the text as to another person. Some say it is like reading in an echo chamber, but others find that it becomes a far more personal encounter with the word. The eyes take in what is on the surface of the page; the ear brings what is said not only within our bodies but into our being. It is easy to look at a text, recognize it at a glance, and react with something equivalent to: "Oh, that reading. I know it. I've done that before." But when you give your undivided attention to a text, and really listen to it, you may find yourself connecting to it in a way that has never happened before. Approach each reading of the word of God as if you are listening to it for the first time.

Wallace Bacon, one of the great teachers of oral interpretation at Northwestern University, would speak of the need to approach a text as an "other," as a "thou," in contrast to thinking of the text as an "it," that is, as something inanimate. Remind yourself that it is truly God trying to address God's people, but for the word to come to full life, to be "Thou" to another, to the Body of Christ gathered for worship, it needs us: our voice, body, mind, emotions, heart, and imagination. The text waits on us to come along to raise it up from the page and transform it from print into purposeful speech.

At any time during this attentive listening, you might find yourself being pulled into prayer. Allow yourself to go where the text is drawing you. Let the word speak to your heart. Dwell with the word. This approach is one form of *lectio divina* or "holy reading" that has been part of the Christian monastic tradition for centuries, going back to St. Benedict and mentioned in his rule: pray, read, meditate, contemplate. This approach to reading appreciates the text as something to be chewed and digested, regurgitated and consumed. Michael Downey in reflecting on *lectio divina* in his book *Trappist* writes: "In *lectio*, the eyes behold, caress, embrace the text. Words are savored, chewed, swallowed slowly. They taste of God. They are like honey in the mouth, gladdening the heart."[13] *Lectio* lets God in and brings us closer to the Mystery at the heart of life.

We find precedence for this in the Bible itself. The prophet Jeremiah was given a scroll to eat and told: "See, I place my words in your mouth" (1:9); later in the book Jeremiah himself says: "When I found your words, I devoured them" (15:16). And in the book of the prophet Ezekiel, a voice says to him: "O mortal, eat what is offered to you; eat this scroll and go, speak to the house of Israel." Ezekiel goes on: "Then I ate it and in my mouth it was as sweet as honey" (Ezek 3:1-3). In the New Testament's book of Revelation a voice from heaven tells the seer to take the scroll from the hand of the angel who stands on the sea and the land, and when the seer stands before him, the angel says: "Take and swallow it. It will turn your stomach sour, but in your mouth it will taste as sweet as honey" (Rev 10:8-11).

The Fathers of the Church continued this imagery of eating the word of God. St. Jerome wrote that we should be like camels rather than horses when it comes to digesting the word of God, not chewing and swallowing but chewing, swallowing, regurgitating, chewing some more, swallowing, regurgitating, and so on. Not a very pretty image but a provocative one and pertinent to emphasizing that the word of God was given to be nourishment, part of the bread of life, sustaining and entering into our very being.

Step Three: Study the Word. As we are reading a text, a number of things begin to happen. We begin to enter into another world. After all, these texts go back thousands of years. We are listening to stories, ideas, and advice from a different culture and time. We are confronted with different customs, styles of communication, genres of literature—sometimes a story or a part of one, at other times an excerpt from a letter, a fragment of a prophetic speech, an apocalyptic vision, or a segment from one of the books of Wisdom literature. In addition, we realize that we are reading only a few verses from a longer work. Different kinds of questions can come up: How do you pronounce this word? What exactly does this word or phrase or sentence mean? What does this whole text mean? How does it fit into the book it came from? Why was it chosen for today? Does it relate to the other readings? Or to the liturgical season? If so, how? This is where study can be helpful. A few resources can help not only to understand a particular reading for the purpose of proclamation but further your own spiritual growth. Let's consider a few of the questions just mentioned.

The pronunciation of words. You have been appointed to do the first reading for Pentecost Sunday, which is the story of the first Pentecost from the Acts of the Apostles: Acts 2:1-11. You are reading it aloud to yourself and moving along quite smoothly. The followers of Jesus are together in one place when suddenly a noise like a strong driving wind fills the house, and there appears tongues as of fire which settle over each one there, and all are filled with the Holy Spirit and begin to speak in tongues. Then we get to the large crowd who hears them, and the text reads:

> We are Parthians, Medes, and Elamites,
> inhabitants of Mesopotamia, Judea and Cappadocia
> Pontus and Asia, Phrygia and Pamphylia,
> Egypt and the districts of Libya and Cyrene. . . .

Elamites? Cappadocia? Mesopotamia? Phrygia? Pamphylia? A handy guide to biblical pronunciation is the small, literally pocket-size, book *Lector's Guide to Biblical Pronunciations, Updated* by Joseph M. Staudacher (see resources), which provides the correct pronunciation and stress for all the puzzling names of persons, places, and things that occur during the three-year Sunday cycle of readings. Thus, Phrygia is rendered FRIH-dzhih-uh and Pamphylia is indicated to be pam-FHIL-ih-uh. The newest edition offers a Sunday by Sunday listing of difficult pronunciations, as well as an alphabetical listing.

Sometimes a problem with a word does not end with its pronunciation. Read the following text for the Twenty-fifth

Sunday in Ordinary Time, C Cycle, from the book of the prophet Amos, who is chastising the dishonest merchants:

> Hear this, you who trample upon the needy
>   and destroy the poor of the land!
> "When will the new moon be over," you ask,
>   "that we may sell our grain,
>   and the Sabbath, that we may display the wheat?
> We will diminish the ephah,
>   add to the shekel,
>   and fix our scales for cheating! . . ." (Amos 8:4-7)

While the *Lector's Guide* will tell you how to pronounce ephah (EE-fuh) and shekel (SHEHK-uhl), you might want to consult a dictionary of the Bible such as John Pilch's *The Cultural Dictionary of the Bible*[14] to find out what these words refer to. Both words come from the ancient world of weights and measures, of scales and balances, which were an essential part of daily life in the time before coins. A shekel comes from the Hebrew verb *shakal* (to weigh, to pay) and the noun shekel refers to a unit of weight; the ephah is a measure of volume. The rage of Amos is aimed at those wealthy merchants who cannot wait for worship to be over so they can cheat on the poor at the marketplace. One can hear—and feel—God's anger simmering within Amos's contemptuous condemnation of their desire to have the Sabbath over and get back to bilking the poor.

It is not only the occasional exotic word that needs further understanding but sometimes a particular geographical setting, such as the desert or wilderness that serves as both the place of God's wooing and testing Israel. Or it may be a title like "suffering servant" of Isaiah or the woman giving birth in the book of Revelation, both of which carry with them layers of meaning, individual and corporate. Behind many of the stories in the Gospels lie such core values of Mediterranean culture as shame, honor, and secrecy. An understanding of purification customs, dietary laws, the various Jewish festivals, the tense relationships between Jews, Samaritans, and Gentiles—all are part of understanding the world from which the biblical texts were born. Even one's understanding of such common Hebrew words like *Abba* and *Shalom* may need to be retuned. Pilch tells us that *Abba* would be better translated as "Father" rather than the frequently heard "Daddy," and *shalom* has at least eight meanings in the Old Testament.[15]

Sometimes study leads not so much to an understanding of what at first sight is strange or even bizarre, but of attaining a deeper awareness of what on first hearing comes across as clear, even obvious. Go back to the reading from First Corinthians and listen to it again. Is there anything that is not understandable? For most readers the proclamation could be read with a fair degree of understanding. But going to a commentary on the Sunday Lectionary can give fresh insight into what Paul is saying.

Preaching the New Lectionary, Year B, by Dianne Bergant with Richard Fragomeni[16] can be very helpful to lectors as well as to preachers. In this instance it tells the reader that the simple line from Paul, "No one can say, 'Jesus is Lord,' except by the Holy Spirit," holds a world of meaning. At first utterance, it seems a fairly straightforward statement. Just say it clearly and move on. The Holy Spirit gives you the ability, better the faith, to call Jesus "Lord." But for the original listeners, to say these three words was both an act of courage as well as one of faith. For subjects of the Roman Empire to say "Jesus is Lord" was a political act. Only Caesar was to be called "Lord," the official title of the Roman Emperor. Anyone who said anyone else was "Lord" could be punished for treason. And that would mean death. Saying Jesus was Lord was also a controversial religious statement. For the Jewish people, which many of the first Christians were, to say "Jesus is Lord" was to give him the recognition that belonged only to YHWH, the one and only God of Israel. This statement was blasphemous to those Jews who were not followers of Jesus and with whom the early Christians still worshiped. So to make this statement was dangerous both politically and religiously, leaving one open to charges of treason and sacrilege. Thus, Paul declares that only the Holy Spirit could give one the faith and the courage to make this dangerous proclamation. Now, note the complexity and richness of the next line of the reading:

> There are different kinds of spiritual gifts but the same Spirit;
> there are different forms of service but the same Lord;

> there are different workings but the same God
> who produces all of them in everyone.
> To each individual the manifestation of the Spirit
> is given for some benefit.

Bergant points out that, while the threefold designation of "gifts," "forms of service," and "workings" would seem to be associated with the Spirit, Son, and Father respectively, the next line, however, places them all as "manifestations" or expressions of the Holy Spirit. What might be of interest to lectors is the range of these manifestations: the "different kinds of spiritual gifts" (*charisma*), Bergant tells us, are related to the working of the Spirit in such instances as speaking in tongues and uttering prophesy, which usually took place within worship; "different forms of service" refer to more humble forms of service to the community, such as waiting on tables, taking up a collection, caring for the widows, etc.; and "different workings" concerns "feats of great energy or divine power." Now all this kind of information cannot be communicated in a reading, but it deepens *your* understanding of what comes under these three distinct categories and calls you to give some weight to each of these designations as you read them. In the end, the point of the passage is found in the final statement that the Spirit is at work in many ways, on many levels, in each individual for the common good, leading the members of the body to deeper unity in worship, work, and wondrous deeds.

A final level of understanding that study can bring is the relationship between the readings and the liturgical season. Once again, *Preaching the New Lectionary* not only provides commentary on each reading but also suggests various themes to help stimulate the imagination of preachers and readers. The seven-volume series *Days of the Lord* also offers helpful reflection on the texts as they relate to the liturgical season. (While not everyone can afford all the resources mentioned here, perhaps a parish might start a small resource library to benefit both lectors and other interested listeners.)

Step Four: Praying with the Word. Throughout this time of spiritual preparation, you might find yourself drawn toward prayer. The end of the word of God, the reason God sends it forth, like the snow and rain that come down, is so that it waters the earth, making it fertile and fruitful, bringing forth a harvest of forty, sixty, and a hundredfold. The word of Jesus is also presented as a word that prunes, cutting off what is dead so more fruit can come forth. The first place (although, sometimes, the last) the word of God may strike is our own heads and hearts, offering us a fresh way of looking at God, our world, and ourselves. Whether you are listening to the word, studying it, or sitting in silence before it, give yourself over to any impulse to pray. The first step in preparation then is spiritual. Before giving expression to the word, allow it to make an impression on you. From such encounters comes fruitful proclamation.

KEEP IN MIND

Preparing to lector involves not only speech preparation but also spiritual preparation:

1. Begin with prayer to the Holy Spirit.
2. Read the text aloud, slowly, digesting it.
3. Study the text with the help of biblical commentaries.
4. Pray with the text in the days before you read it to the community.

Speaking Preparation

> A speaking style on the part of readers that is audible, clear, and intelligent is the first means of transmitting the word of God properly to the congregation. (LMIn, 13)

Reading at Mass is an act of public address. It is a speech act, even though the words you speak are not your own. They are recognized and accepted by the Church as "The word of the Lord." And so, it is crucial that the word of God be proclaimed in a style of speaking that communicates. A mistaken assumption is that if a person can read, he or she can read at Mass. And so someone coming into church might be asked: "Would you do one of the readings this morning?" This is not fair, either to those asked, (even if they are lectors, they need to prepare), or to the community, or to the word of God. It is not that a person may not be capable of doing a reading after a quick "once-over" in the sacristy, especially if one has experience as a lector. At the minimum most experienced readers will be loud and clear, but to what degree the reading will be "intelligent" is another question. And, even more to the point, to what degree will this reading reflect that "warm and living love and knowledge of the Scripture" Pope Paul VI called for?

The discipline of oral interpretation is helpful for expressing the demands that reading a text in public makes. Charlotte Lee, an early leading figure in this performance discipline at Northwestern University, in one of the earliest works published on the art of oral interpretation, defined it as "the art of communicating to an audience a work of literary art in its intellectual, emotional, and aesthetic entirety."[17] Such an understanding calls for time spent with a reading to discover its meaning, both intellectually and emotionally, that is, its "mind's-truth" as well as its "heart's-truth," along with coming to terms with the various aesthetic aspects that distinguish one genre or type of biblical literature from another. All three dimensions—intellectual, emotional, and aesthetic—influence how a text is read. The area of aesthetics concerns the particular qualities that help to make the various books of the Bible works of beauty, leading so many readers to regard the Bible as literature as well as a book of faith. For lectors, this has to do with recognizing the different qualities that distinguish a story from a letter or a prophetic utterance, the difference between reading prose and poetry. This area of the different genres found in the Bible will be taken up shortly.

Wallace Bacon helps us realize that every text demands a personal commitment from the reader.[18] The relationship between a reader and the text can be superficial or intimate. This will depend on the degree of connection that occurs. Bacon calls for a *coalescence* to take place between a reader and a text, that is, a certain "growing together" that occurs only when a reader and a text enter into communion. He invites us to think of both the reader and the poem as having an outer form and an inner form. For the reader the outer form is what you see and hear—face, body, voice—whereas the inner form includes the reader's thoughts and feelings. The text also has an outer form composed of the print on the page, the words that lie there waiting to be translated into speech, while the inner form is the thoughts, feelings, and the way a piece moves and breathes.

In the act of interpreting a text in a way that communicates, there must be a coming together of the inner form of the text and the inner form of the reader. Readers give themselves to the text so that, through their efforts, the text may be heard and felt and known. The text yields its inner thoughts and feelings to the reader, opening up its inner world and beauty to the attentiveness of the reader. Bacon goes as far as saying, "It is perhaps not too much to suggest that there is a kind of love relationship between reader and poem, each reaching out to the other."[19] When this fails to happen, we have only the meeting of outer forms.

Perhaps you can recall a reading or a lecture where the speaker was not engaged. We even describe the experience with words like "his heart wasn't in it" or "she just didn't seem to connect with what she was saying." The words of a text can become the words spoken by a reader without going any deeper. To a listener, it sounds rather hollow because what is said is not thought or felt. In her study bringing together oral interpretation theory and the theology of the Incarnation, Alla Bozarth-Campbell wrote that "the ideal interpretation may be defined as the full revelation of whatever experience is inherent in the literature."[20] We discover what that experience is when we spend time with the text, befriending it, becoming intimate with it so that we know it as a living being, a "thou" rather than an "it." We are called to love the word, but love only flows from knowledge. And communicating the word flows from the union of knowledge and love and skill. A final image comes from Jerzy Grotowski, the director of an experimental Polish theater group in the 1970s, who spoke of the "holy interpreter" who lays down his/her life for the text. By yielding one's body, mind, heart, and spirit to the sacred text, one dies to oneself so that the text might live.

We will consider three areas important for the public proclamation of the text: the requirements of the text, the requirements of the listener, and the requirements of the space. As you are going along, you might begin to think to yourself: "How am I ever going to remember all this?" You won't. But over time, you will begin to absorb these various aspects. What is being done here is to try to set out as fully as possible what makes a good reading of God's word.

The requirements of the text. The first suggestion is to read all the biblical texts slowly and prayerfully. Start with the gospel, then with the first and second reading. Don't forget to read the responsorial psalm and the alleluia verse, too. This will take you into the biblical world for this particular Sunday. During the liturgical seasons of Advent, Christmas, Lent, and Easter, the principle of harmony of theme is often at work, and a slow reading of all the texts will help you to begin seeing some of the common links. During Ordinary Time the first reading has been chosen to be in harmony with the gospel, so reading the gospel first will help you to identify what should be emphasized in the first reading. The second reading during Ordinary Time is on its own track and was not chosen to correspond with the other readings, although there are times when a satisfying complementarity can be found.

Each text is unique, offering a particular experience or thought to the listener. But there are also certain *genres*, or types of readings, that share characteristics appropriate to their form. Among the genres lectors commonly encounter are the story, the letter, and the poem. Each of these has its demands. Not only do the stories found in the Lectionary interweave a story-teller and particular characterizations, move from point A to point B to point C, usually build to a climax, and have varying demands in terms of pacing and energy level, but often a reader is plunged into the middle of the story and will need to have some sense of the larger narrative and how this segment fits into it. The readings from the letters, especially those of St.

Paul, not only call for lectors to be conscious of the community's ability to absorb abstract theological content, calling for skillful phrasing and careful consideration of pacing. Often sentences are lengthy, complex, and even convoluted in a way that threatens a listener's understanding. The poetic form occurs in the oracles and speeches of the prophets, the psalms, and often in that body of work we call wisdom literature. Powerful images and emotional force are qualities at the heart of most poetry. The poetry of the Scriptures has certain aesthetic characteristics like parallelism and a poetic rhythm based on a certain number of stresses per line. While every reading has its own demands, a look at some of the general demands of each genre may be of help.

a. *The Story*

There are wonderful stories to be found in the Lectionary. Or, more accurately, there are wonderful fragments of stories in the Lectionary: the confrontation between God and Adam and Eve in the garden, Noah being given a rainbow as a sign of the covenant, Abraham being told to look up and try to count the stars as a sign of God's promise, Moses talking to a bush, David being tempted to thrust his spear into the sleeping body of King Saul, the mighty general Naaman plunging into the Jordan seven times and emerging with the flesh of a little child, and Jonah preaching a message of doom in Nineveh and getting instant results. These stories call us to use our imagination and story-telling skills.

Consider the first reading from the Acts of the Apostles (10:25-26, 34-35, 44-48), selected for the Sixth Sunday of Easter, B Cycle, a story about the visit of Peter to the house of a Gentile named Cornelius. In the Lectionary you find the reading presented as follows:

A reading from the Acts of the Apostles

When Peter entered, Cornelius met him
  and, falling at his feet, paid him homage.
Peter, however, raised him up, saying,
  "Get up. I myself am also a human being."

>Then Peter proceeded to speak and said,
>>"In truth, I see that God shows no partiality.
>Rather, in every nation whoever fears him and acts uprightly
>>is acceptable to him."

>When Peter was still speaking these things,
>>the Holy Spirit fell upon all who were listening to the word.
>The circumcised believers who had accompanied Peter
>>were astounded that the gift of the Holy Spirit
>>should have been poured out on the Gentiles also,
>>>for they could hear them speaking in tongues and
>>>>glorifying God.
>Then Peter responded,
>>"Can anyone withhold the water for baptizing these people,
>>who have received the Holy Spirit even as we have?"
>He ordered them to be baptized in the name of Jesus Christ.

>The word of the Lord

A story, however brief, has movement: a beginning, middle, and an end. This story begins with Peter entering the home of someone named Cornelius and goes on to tell us what happens once he gets inside. When you are dealing with a story, it is good to ask yourself some questions: Do I understand the movement of the story, what is happening here? Does this story have a clear beginning, middle, and end. Does the story have a turning point? a climax? Who are the characters in the story? Do they speak? If so, how do they say what they say, that is, what are the feelings under the words? If not, are their cues within the narrative to convey a character's condition? Are there any words or expressions that carry special meaning (as "Lord" did in the 1 Corinthians reading mentioned earlier)?

The first thing to notice is how this reading plunges you into the middle of the action. It begins by saying, "When Peter entered, Cornelius met him." Entered where? Cornelius who? Why is he there? The text as presented in the Lectionary does not say! This reading also leaves out some verses within the excerpt given: Acts 10:27-33 and 36-43. What happens in these verses? Sometimes verses are omitted that confuse or are unclear, but in this case, these verses are part of the story, and would summarize some of what had already happened before the present text begins. So, have a Bible at hand. Read the missing verses. But here even more is necessary because the story itself begins twenty-four verses earlier. The selection for this Sunday is the final scene in what can be thought of as a three-act play.

The two scenes leading to Peter entering the house of Cornelius tell us first about Cornelius, a Roman centurion stationed at Caesarea, who is both devout and "God-fearing," that is, a Gentile who had come to believe in the God of Israel. Cornelius has a vision in which an angel tells him God has heard his prayer and that he should send to Joppa for a man named Simon Peter. Then the story switches to Joppa where Peter, staying at the house of Simon, the tanner, goes up on the roof and has a vision. In this vision a huge curtain descends bearing all kinds of four-legged creatures and a voice tells Peter, "Kill and eat." He balks at this command and the voice has to tell him the same thing three times, and then. . . . As you can see, you really need to read the entire story to appreciate the full impact of this Sunday's reading.

Knowing what has already happened helps you to have the background for why Peter is entering the house of Cornelius. But more is necessary to understand how to interpret Peter's reaction when Cornelius falls at his feet: "Get up. I myself am also a human being." Here it is helpful to know something about the beliefs and customs of Jews and Gentiles. Even though Peter's vision told him to go to the house of Cornelius, as a devout Jew, Peter would have been brought up to consider it unlawful to cross the threshold of any Gentile. The Law of Moses considered Gentiles ritually unclean (as explained in the missing vv. 27-33). Furthermore, to have a Gentile fall on his knees was an act of homage shown only to a god. So Peter's reaction would be immediate and strong, capturing someone unsettled and upset at this greeting: "Get up. I myself am also a human being."

Peter goes on to speak about what he learned from his experience on the roof at Joppa: "God shows no partiality. Rather, in every nation, whoever fears him and acts uprightly is acceptable to him." Peter starts to preach (you will find his sermon in the missing vv. 36-43) but as he is preaching, "the Holy Spirit fell

upon all who were listening to the word." This is the high point of
the story. Every story has one, so look for it. These Gentiles were
not yet baptized. The time for the Holy Spirit to come would be at
their baptism, but on this occasion Peter is still preaching to them
about Jesus when "the Holy Spirit fell upon all who were listening." A sense of wonder and amazement should characterize this
moment in the reading. It reminds us that God cannot wait to get
hold of us, to enter our lives, to draw us into the divine life. Peter
responds accordingly by baptizing them immediately.

Another instance of coming into the middle of a story occurs
in the reading from Genesis 3:9-15, 20, selected for the feast of
the Immaculate Conception of the Blessed Virgin Mary. The excerpt begins after the man and woman have eaten from the
fruit of the tree; they are hiding from God who is "walking
about in the garden at the time of the evening breeze." The
Lord God calls out to the man and asks him, "Where are you?"
When they finally come out, Adam says he was afraid because
he was naked, so he hid. God then asks: "Who told you that
you were naked? You have eaten then from the tree of which I
had forbidden you to eat!" How one says this last sentence can
vary. A reader might choose to portray an angry God, furious at
the act of disobedience. Or you might present God as cool and
collected, calmly summing up what happened. Or perhaps
something in the middle: a God who is miffed, mildly annoyed.
Reading the whole story can help a reader decide; reading a
good commentary might help even more.

In his commentary on Genesis biblical scholar Walter
Brueggemann[21] reminds us that often we think of the God por-
trayed in Genesis 2–3 simply as the God of prohibition, the God
who forbade Adam and Eve to eat from the tree of the knowledge of good and evil that was in the garden. But the God presented in this story is first of all the God of *vocation*, who calls the
human creature and entrusts to him (Eve is not yet on the scene)
the care of the garden, to till and keep it (2:15); secondly, God is
the God of *permission*, who allows the creature "to eat from any
of the trees in the garden" (2:16). It is only after these first two actions on God's part that we hear the God of the prohibition
speak: ". . . except from the tree of the knowledge of good and

evil; the day you eat from it you will die" (2:17). In telling this story of creation, the God who created is the God who called and permitted and only then forbade. This God might well be presented as heartbroken when saying: "You have eaten, then, from the tree from which I had forbidden you to eat."

The problem of reading only fragments of biblical stories is recognized in the Introduction to the Lectionary when it allows for "concise introductions before the readings, *especially the first*" (15; italics mine). Such introductions should be "simple, faithful to the text, brief, well prepared, and properly varied to suit the text they introduce" (15). Reading the biblical stories is an invitation to create for the community brief encounters with the major figures of the Judaeo-Christian story. Finally, some lectors worry about "overdoing" or overacting a story. While granting that this may occur, I find more readings are under-read than over-acted. Search out the inner truth of these characters in the humanity we share with them. Emotions like anger, hurt, fear, love, jealousy should register in a reading, even when they are attributed to God. Don't let fear of overdoing it lock you into a lifeless, dispassionate reading of a story that is meant to be life-giving for the community.

b. *The Letter*

Every Sunday and feast day there is a reading from one of the letters, most often from the writings of St. Paul. Occasionally there is something from the other letters: James is read for five weeks during Year B and the letters of Peter and John are featured during the Easter and Christmas seasons, respectively. The First Letter to the Corinthians is spread over the three-year cycle, while the Letter to the Hebrews (which most scholarly works recognize as a homily by an unknown author) is divided between Years B and C. The second readings during Ordinary Time are semi-continuous and are deliberately brief so as to be easily grasped by listeners. (One might ask whether they are often too brief, barely making much of an impression at all? Is the attention span of the contemporary congregation really so attenuated by watching television with its frequent commercials that people can not listen for more than a minute or two?)

A lector will find it helpful to have some knowledge of the letter's background: some information about the community to whom Paul was writing, his relationship with them, and what the situation was that evoked or provoked the letter. While the Corinthians were a cantankerous and divisive group and the Galatians provoked Paul's angriest words on record, the Philippians had a special place in his heart, and the Romans received some of his most eloquent words. Furthermore, being aware of the structure of the letter and where a particular passage is taken from can help a lector read with greater understanding. The brief introduction before each of the letters in the New American Bible offers a helpful overview of both the letter and its structures. For greater depth, look for a good commentary on the particular letter.

Paul's letters usually begin with a formal greeting followed by a thanksgiving, then the author launches into his instruction which lasts most of the letter, laying out the theological vision he wishes to impart to the community, or discussing problems that have come to his attention. In this first part of the letter, we find Paul doing all he can to set out the groundwork for what it means to be in Christ. The final chapters usually offer practical advice for daily life within the community and in the larger world. Some letters have a very personal tone, for instance, those addressed to the Philippians, Corinthians, Galatians, Thessalonians, and to Philemon (the only private letter that has come down to us), while others are more formal, such as Romans, Colossians, and Ephesians.

One important characteristic that marks most of the excerpts read from letters is a certain *density of thought*. Paul was schooled in rabbinic thought, and his letters reflect his developing theological understanding of what it meant to enter into the mystery of Christ, to be "in Christ." So, give yourself time to understand what Paul is saying, and give your listeners time to absorb his thought. This does not mean a torturously slow reading, but a reader must take into account how important pausing and good phrasing can be for listener comprehension when a reading is offering some very profound theological concepts. These readings are often more "weighty" because they are more abstract, and the pace needs to be more deliberate than when telling a story.

Consider the opening lines from the Letter of St. Paul to the Romans (5:12-19) on the First Sunday of Lent, Cycle A:

> Brothers and sisters:
> Through one man sin entered the world,
>   and through sin, death,
>   and thus death came to all men, inasmuch as
>   all sinned—
>   for up to the time of the law, sin was in the world,
>   though sin is not accounted when there is no law.
> But death reigned from Adam to Moses,
>   even over those who did not sin,
>   after the pattern of the trespass of Adam,
>   who is the type of the one who was to come.

That is not an easy reading to grasp on first hearing. And the reading goes on in this vein for another seven verses. (True, you might opt for the shorter version of this reading offered as an alternative; but don't make this move too quickly. This is one of the great Pauline passages in what is arguably his greatest letter.) Romans is Paul's masterpiece, and it is worth all our effort to read it in a way that is "audible, clear, and intelligent" as the Introduction to the Lectionary asks. Such a reading involves a number of the factors we will discuss in the next section under the requirements of the listener; for now, suffice it to say that certain readings have a density of thought that calls for careful preparation.

There is also in many of the letters a *density of feeling*. What I love about Paul is his passion. One might imagine him banging his hand against the desk in frustration as he writes to the Galatians: "I am amazed that you are so quickly forsaking the one who called you by the grace of Christ for a different gospel— not that there is another!" (1:6-7a). Later on in that same letter he writes, "O stupid Galatians! Who has bewitched you. . . ." (3:1). Or there is his gentle manipulation, all for the sake of the gospel, of course, in the Letter to Philemon where he is trying to convince the wealthy Philemon, his friend, to forgive and take back the runaway slave Onesimus—a crime punishable by death—"no longer as a slave but more than a slave, a brother, beloved especially to me, but even more so to you, as a man and in the Lord. So if you regard me as a partner, welcome him as you would me" (16-17). Paul pulls out all the stops in this letter and we find here that gospel seed that will eventually take root and topple the institution of slavery.

For one of the most eloquent and feeling-full expressions of Paul's thought, turn again to Romans 8:37-39 and read the text of the second reading for the Eighteenth Sunday, Cycle A:

> Brothers and Sisters:
> Who will separate us from the love of Christ?
> Will anguish, or distress, or persecution, or famine,
>   or nakedness, or peril, or the sword?
> No, in all these things we conquer overwhelmingly
>   through him who loved us.
> For I am convinced that neither death, nor life,
>   nor angels, nor principalities,
>   nor present things, nor future things,
>   nor powers, nor height, nor depth,
>   nor any other creature will be able to separate us
>   from the love of God in Christ Jesus our Lord.

If you can read this in a dispassionate fashion, in a dry, distilled, emotionless near monotone (as it is sometimes read), if you can read this without feeling to some degree caught up in the passionate love of Christ for all men and women, if you can read this without feeling within your heart some degree of the urgency Paul felt to convey God's love in Christ to a church he has never visited, then please *don't* read it. Let someone else do it. I am not calling for over-emoting in a way that calls attention to the reader, but often lectors are so afraid of overdoing it, that they barely do it. To quote the most frequently heard word of advice in the New Testament: "Fear not." Both density of thought and feeling are found in the letters and need to be communicated.

Another challenge in Paul's letters comes in effectively communicating a series of brief exhortations or a listing of various attributes or names. An example of the former can be found in the second reading on the Third Sunday of Advent, Cycle B from the First Letter to the Thessalonians (5:16ff.):

Brothers and Sisters:
Rejoice always. Pray without ceasing.
In all circumstances, give thanks,
   for this is the will of God for you in Christ Jesus.
Do not quench the Spirit.
Do not despise prophetic utterances.
Test everything; retain what is good.
Refrain from every kind of evil.

With this kind of listing, consider each command a seed that you are planting in the consciousness of the community. Give each one a moment to sink in. The other kind of listing, a series of names or attributes, can be found above in the selection from Romans 8, which contains two listings of names; or look at the opening of the second reading for the feast of The Holy Family, Cycle A, for a listing of various attributes. At the beginning of this selection from the Letter to the Colossians (3:12), we read:

Put on, as God's chosen ones, holy and beloved,
   heartfelt compassion, kindness, humility, gentleness, patience,
   bearing with one another and forgiving one another . . .

If you rattle through these qualities like a laundry list, people will not have time to absorb them. Again, consider each of these qualities as seeds to be sown in the minds of your listeners: "Put on heartfelt compassion. . . , kindness. . . , humility . . . . gentleness . . . . patience. . . ." Don't rush. Give people a moment to absorb each of them. When preparing, you might think of an example of each quality; that will help color your expression. And watch for falling into either a singsong pattern or a monotone.

One final note: the liturgical context or occasion can make a difference as to how the same text is heard. For instance, Romans 6:3-5 is read at the Easter Vigil, at a celebration of the baptism of children held on a Sunday afternoon, the funeral of a loved one, or a Sunday during Ordinary Time. Each setting would effect how this reading is heard:

Are you unaware that we who were baptized into Christ Jesus
   were baptized into his death?

> We were indeed buried with him through baptism into death,
>> so that, just as Christ was raised from the dead
>> by the glory of the Father,
>> we too might live in newness of life.
> For if we have grown into union with him through a death like his,
>> We shall also be united with him in the resurrection.

c. *Prophecy*

During the three-year Sunday cycle, we hear some prophetic texts in all the liturgical seasons. Isaiah is read most frequently, especially at Advent and Christmas. Lent has several prophetic readings during the later Sundays of the season, whereas, during the Easter season, apart from the Easter Vigil, there are no readings from the prophets since the first reading on Sunday is always from the Acts of the Apostles. Sundays in Ordinary Time, however, feature a variety of prophetic texts, chosen to correspond to or parallel the gospel reading. In the readings for the two-year weekday cycle, there is a rich selection from many of the prophetic books, with Daniel and many of the minor prophets read during Year One and the major prophets—Isaiah, Jeremiah, Ezekiel, Amos, Hosea—and the remaining minor prophets read during Year Two.

Several features call for the reader's attention. While there are some narratives in the prophetic selections, as on the Fourth Sunday of Advent, Cycle A, when Isaiah confronts King Ahaz with his dissembling before God and utters the familiar words, "the virgin shall conceive, and bear a son, and shall name him Emmanuel" (7:14), most of the prophetic texts are presented as poetic utterances with little sense of their historical framework. As has been mentioned, this is because these texts are chosen to correspond in some way with the gospel and to point towards Christ. The first thing a lector will want to do is to read the gospel. Then, watch for how the words of the prophet fit either into the particular liturgical season or connect with the gospel of Ordinary Time.

Because the prophetic word is cast in the form of poetic utterance, deep feeling and strong emotions mark these texts. Listen to the words of Hosea (2:16b, 17b, 21-22) on the Eighth Sunday in Ordinary Time, Cycle B:

Thus says the Lord:
I will lead her into the desert
  and speak to her heart.
She will respond there as in the days of her youth,
  when she came up from the land of Egypt.
I will espouse you to me forever.
  I will espouse you in right and in justice,
  in love and in mercy;
I will espouse you in fidelity,
  and you shall know the Lord.

Or hear the strong words of Jeremiah addressed to God (20:7-9), objecting to how he has been *seduced, enticed,* or *overpowered* by God; these are the words used in other translations instead of the weaker *duped* that is found in the New American Bible translation on the Twenty-second Sunday in Ordinary Time, Cycle A:

You duped me, O Lord, and I let myself be duped;
  you were too strong for me, and you triumphed.
All day long I am an object of laughter;
  everyone mocks me.

Whenever I speak, I must cry out,
  violence and outrage is my message;
The word of the Lord has brought me
  derision and reproach all the day.

I say to myself, I will not mention him,
  I will speak in his name no more.
But then it become like fire burning in my heart,
  imprisoned in my bones;
I grow weary holding it in, I cannot endure it.

What are the appropriate emotions a lector needs to convey so that this reading registers in its "intellectual, emotional, and aesthetic entirety"?

Sometimes the prophets rail in anger as Amos does against the wealthy "lying upon beds of ivory, stretched comfortably on their couches," eating and drinking and listening to harps, while they exploit the poor and the weak:

> Therefore, now they shall be the first to go into exile,
>   and their wanton revelry shall be done away with.
>   (Twenty-Sixth Sunday, Cycle C, Amos 6:1a, 4-7)

And toward the end of the church year we hear passages that offer visions of the Day of the Lord, such as the words of the prophet Daniel who saw "one like a Son of man coming, on the clouds of heaven" (Christ the King, Cycle B) or the visionary of the book of Revelation who paints a portrait of

> . . . a great multitude,
> which no one could count,
> from every nation, race, people, and tongue.
> They stood before the throne and before the Lamb,
>   wearing while robes and holding palm branches in their hands.
> They cried out in a loud voice:
>   "Salvation comes from our God, who is seated on the throne,
>   and from the Lamb . . ."
>   (Solemnity of All Saints, Rev 7:2-4, 9-14)

Such texts speak to the heart and the imagination as much as to the mind. They come from the heart of God, addressed to the heart of a people constantly in need of reformation. We who read these texts are the instruments through whom God continues to sing the divine love song to the world. Our work is to read in such a way as to evoke awe, wonder, praise, repentance, and thanksgiving.

d. *Wisdom Literature*

The writings from Wisdom literature were among the last of the Old Testament books written. The three-year Sunday cycle includes selections from Job (2), Proverbs (3), Ecclesiastes (1), Wisdom (8), and Sirach (7). These selections can be rather difficult to get on a first hearing, due to complicated syntax and the density characteristic of poetic expression, so take care to allow time for the thoughts and images to register. Consider the opening lines from the book of Wisdom (6:12-13) on the Thirty-second Sunday, A:

Resplendent and unfading is wisdom,
and she is readily perceived by those who love her,
and found by those who seek her.
She hastens to make herself known in anticipation of their desire;
whoever watches for her at dawn shall be not disappointed,
for he shall find her sitting by his gate.

These are not difficult lines to read when you consider them line by line, but they need to be given room to stretch out and settle into our understanding, especially the beginning segment of each sentence.

More difficult, if not downright incomprehensible on a first hearing, is the opening sentence from the book of Wisdom (12:13) on the Sixteenth Sunday of the Year, Cycle A:

There is no god besides you who have the care of all,
that you need show you have not unjustly condemned.

And it goes on in a similar vein. This is a challenging text for reader and listeners, and a little warning beforehand to listen with full attention might be suggested. But the ending (12:19) is quite beautiful, a reward for sticking with it:

And you taught your people, by these deeds,
that those who are just must be kind;
and you gave your children good ground for hope
that you would permit repentance for their sins.

These texts invite us to share in the wisdom of the Jewish tradition handed down for over two thousand years. We want to read them in a way that sends listeners to these books for further instruction.

e. *The Responsorial Psalm*

The psalms are an integral part of the Liturgy of the Word, an important part of the prayer life of the Church, and a link between the Jewish and Christian peoples, binding together these two branches of the family of Abraham. The psalms speak of the longings of the human heart and the many ways it reaches out to make contact with the God who created and redeemed us. A story online recently told of the ongoing power of these ancient prayers. On the day following a bomb explosion on a bus in Jerusalem, which killed seventeen people and wounded about sixty others, a young man was found reading the psalms in the bus shelter next to where the explosion had occurred. He said he believed that by reciting the psalms he could help stop the violence. He pointed to Psalm 124 and read the lines: "If God had not been there for us . . . when men rose up against us, then they would have swallowed us up alive by their violent anger," but he went on to say it was a later line that gave him hope: "Blessed be the Lord who has not given us as prey to their teeth."

Fr. Gerard Sloyan reminds us that the psalms are the lyrics of songs.[22] In the liturgy, the psalms should be sung as a rule (LMIn, 20), either responsorially (the cantor sings the verse and the community the response line) or directly (either the cantor or the community sings the psalm straight through, with no response line after each verse). When it is not sung, it should be kept in mind that it is a prayer and "recited in a way that is conducive to meditating on the word of God" (LMIn, 22). Both when said and particularly when sung, the psalms call for careful articulation and a deliberate pace. As a form of poetry, appealing to the senses through rich imagery and rhythmic language, they are meant to stir up our feelings to praise God, lament our failures, voice our questions, declare our needs—even permitting us to ask God, "Why have you abandoned me?" The psalms give us words and images to cry out to God in joy and pain.

There are two particular characteristics of the psalms that require a reader's attention: parallelism and rhythm. As part of the aesthetic quality of Hebrew poetry, both have to do with the experience of "return." Parallelism provides a return of thought; rhythm provides a return of stress or beat. We will deal with parallelism here and with rhythm in the next section. Parallelism is found when two lines express the same thought. Synonymous parallelism has the same thought expressed in different words:

> Where can I go from your spirit,
>> from your presence where can I flee? (Ps 139:7)

Antithetic parallelism repeats a thought but in an opposite way:

> Trust in the Lord with all your heart
> on your own intelligence, rely not. (Prov 3:5)

Being attentive to parallelism in the psalms can help a reader to recognize what phrases needed to be grouped together for easier understanding.

The psalms are one of the great expressions of the Jewish soul. In a reflection on prayer, Rabbi Herbert Bronstein recently quoted the rabbi of Kotsk's reply to his students when asked why he prayed: "I pray to remind myself that I have a soul."[23] In praying the psalms publicly, the reader helps to draw the community into an awareness of its soul, not only as individuals but as a community who longs for God as the deer longs for running water, who walks in the valley of death but fears no evil, who will gather on that holy mountain where every tear will be wiped away and where they will see face to face the living God.

These are the major genres or literary forms that lectors encounter Sunday after Sunday, weekdays, and on most occasions: the story, the letter, and the poem as found in the prophetic word, the word of wisdom, and the psalm. The effective lector is sensitive to the particular requirements of the text that flow from the unique integration of its content and form. But in addition to the requirements of the text, the lector must also be responsive to the requirements of the listeners. To these we now turn.

KEEP IN MIND

- To communicate a work of literary art "in its intellectual, emotional, and aesthetic entirety" demands a personal commitment from the lector.

- The lector is called to be a "holy interpreter" who lays down his/her life for the text, dying to self by giving one's body, mind, heart, and spirit so that the text might live.

- Lectors deal with various literary genres—the story, the letter, and the poem.

- Each makes its own demands on the reader. Some suggestions:

Story: If only a fragment, read the full story. Watch for: the movement of the story and where it builds to a climax; the interplay of narrator and characters; the emotions of the characters: anger, hurt, fear, love, jealousy, confusion, wonder, suspicion. Don't let fear of overdoing it lock you into a lifeless reading.

Letter: See what you can learn about the letter's background: its audience, Paul's relationship with them and the situation that provoked the letter. Watch for a letter's density of thought and feeling. Give listeners time to absorb complicated thought often expressed in complicated sentence structures.

Poetry: While often found in three forms in Scripture: prophecy, wisdom literature, and psalms, poetry speaks to the heart and the imagination as well as the mind. Be sensitive to the imagery and feelings poetry expresses. Prophetic oracles and wisdom literature are often chosen in light of the gospel, so read the gospel first. Listen for rhythm and watch for parallelism in the psalms.

The requirements of the listener. Understanding the text is the first challenge facing a reader. The second is to make sure that the listener understands the reader. A number of areas need attention for listeners to truly hear the word.

a. *The Quality of the Speaking Voice*

The sound that comes forth when we speak can either help or distract listeners from hearing the message. Some people talk in a nasal, whiney manner. In this regard there is no such thing as a good whine. If you find that when you hold your nostrils shut, you can barely speak, there is a good chance that you are talking through your nose. You should be able to pinch your nose shut and still speak in a full voice—try it. Others talk from the back of their throat and can sound like they are on the verge of gargling. In both cases, the vocal quality distracts from the message.

Years ago I studied with a wonderful teacher, Clifford Jackson, who had taught at the American Academy of Dramatic Arts for over twenty-five years. He introduced me to what was called the "chewing method," a technique for relaxing the throat so that the sound would come from the body. While chewing a piece of bread, students were encouraged to make nonsense sounds, using a wide range of voice while doing this, "playing" with sound, as an infant does when learning to speak, keeping the tongue flexible, the jaw loose. While feeling somewhat silly at first, I found that the goal was to have the voice settle into the body rather than in the back of the throat or in the nasal passage. Another helpful exercise was to sing the notes of the scale: do, re, mi, fa, sol, la, ti, do. Then to do this again, but stopping at each note to sing the following words: kah, kay, kee, koh, ku. Jackson explained that the consonant "k," pronounced firmly, parts the vocal folds and allows for a fuller sound to come from the body.

Having a full voice depends most of all on breathing from the diaphragm rather than shallow breathing from the chest. Think of your body as a resonating instrument. You are bringing air into the body to achieve a full sound, as with a clarinet or an oboe. It is not so much a matter of projecting or "throwing" your voice out to the furthest point, but rather of bringing those furthest away toward you to share the thoughts and feelings of a text.

The sound of the voice also is related to posture. If you slouch over the ambo or bend your head too much toward your chest when reading, which can easily happen if you are tall and if the book sits low on the ambo or simply when the text is at the bottom of the page, you are liable to choke off the sound. Better to pick up the book and have it at a level where you can easily drop your eyes. Make sure you are standing straight, not rigid, but with your weight distributed on both legs and not putting more of your weight on one leg. You might imagine yourself as a tree, sending down your roots into the earth.

b. *Vocal Variety*

A common sin against good public reading is monotony, often caused by speaking in a monotone, that is, staying on one note during most of the reading and dropping your voice only at the end of a sentence or phrase. Sometimes this is worsened by dropping a half-step at the end of the phrase, so you sound sad or tired. You can also be monotonous when you use the same pattern of notes over and over again, sometimes this falls into a "sing-song" pattern and listeners find themselves attending more to the melody than the meaning of what is being said.

Vocal variety begins with having a sense of the range of your voice. Think of it as a musical instrument. Range can vary, but most of us have anywhere from an octave and half to a two octave range. (An octave is an eight note scale. When we sing the scale—do, re, mi, fa, sol, la, ti, do—we are covering an octave.) To have a two-octave speaking voice is a range of more than sixteen notes, not counting additional half steps. In music these half steps are called sharps or flats. Usually in speaking we do not use our entire vocal range. As a matter of fact, most of us settle for a fairly narrow speaking range.

Consider when you are on the phone. Most of the time phone conversation is not only quiet but done in an intimate manner, trying not disturb others. Our voice stays within a rather narrow range of a few notes on the scale. But there are those times when someone says something that upsets or surprises you. What does your voice do? Often it will jump into its upper range and ride the vowel sounds of the words, stretching a syllable over several notes. Consider how you might say the following sentences: "NO!! YOU'VE GOT TO BE KIDDING!!!!!" The great actress Dame Edith Evans was noted for her performance as Lady Bracknell in Oscar Wilde's play, *The Importance of Being Earnest*, particularly for one moment in the third act when it is revealed that, as a child, the young hero was found in Paddington Station in a handbag—to which Evans is said to have used every possible note in a two octave range to express her shock, surprise, and total disbelief when saying: "A handbag?"

c. *Rhythm*

Not all words are equal in a sentence. Some syllables are stressed while others are unstressed. Take that last sentence. If we were to mark it with stress and non-stress markings, it would look like this. (Stressed syllables are marked with a dash, unstressed with a dot.)

—   •   —   •   — • •   —   •

Some are stressed while others are unstressed.

If you are reading too quickly, you might mark it this way:

•   •   •   •   •   •   •   •

Some are stressed while others are unstressed.

or if too slowly:

—   —   ——   —— — – — –   —

Some are stressed while others are unstressed

In the last two instances above, you have the case of making nothing important (• • • • •), running through the phrase at warp speed, and then of making everything important (— — —), dragging out the phrase by making each syllable equally important. We also do this when we pronounce the long vowel sound in words like "a" (ay) or "the" (thee), making a word that should be unstressed into a stressed word. A common instance would be to announce a reading by saying: "*Ay* reading from . . . ." instead of "*Uh* reading from . . . ." or, "A reading from the Letter of St. Paul to *thee* Corinthians" instead of ". . . to theh Corinthians."

Good speech can be conducted. Speech is more interesting when there is a variety of interplay between stressed and unstressed syllables. Rhythm can be found in every sentence we speak but this is especially true of poetry. The poetry of the psalms is usually characterized by a certain number of beats in each line, usually three or four. Say aloud these lines from Psalm 96. Can you feel the beat of each line?

/ • • / • / /
Sing to the Lord a new song;

/ • • / / • /
sing to the Lord, all you lands.

/ • • / / • /
Sing to the Lord, bless his name;

```
  •    /    •  •   /  •    /   •  •   /
```
announce his salvation, day after day.

Each line has four beats in it. Or listen to Psalm 85:

```
  /    •    •    /    •    /
```
Kindness and truth shall meet;

```
  /    •    •    /    •    /
```
justice and peace shall kiss.

In these lines you can hear three beats when you read them aloud. As with poetry in the English language, this is not an ironclad rule and sometimes you will only have two stresses in a line, or, on the other side, as many as five stresses. The occasional irregularity of the number of stresses in a line provides variety and prevents monotony. The translators have tried to keep the rhythm of the original Hebrew in which the prayers were written. A similar presence of rhythm can be found in many of the readings from the prophets and in much of the wisdom literature.

In prose, there is a different kind of rhythm, more irregular. But where the stress falls remains important for making the meaning clear. To communicate intelligibly the meaning of the letters of St. Paul and the Gospel of John, readers must watch for putting the stress on the right word, being attentive especially for the oppositions and contrasts often found in these works. Consider the following lines from the Gospel of John on the Sixth Sunday of Easter, A:

> I will not leave you orphans; I will come to you.
> In a little while the world will no longer see me,
>   but you will see me, because I live and you will live.
> On that day you will realize that I am in my Father
>   and you are in me and I am in you.

The first line above is fairly straightforward, emphasizing what Christ will and will not do. You need only emphasize the first "I," but not the second. It is sufficient to say the second "I" clearly but put the stress on the verb "come" in that phrase.

> *I* will *not leave* you *orphans*; I will *come* to you.

The second line, however, must be seen as a contrast to the third
line:

> In the little while the *world* will *no longer see* me,
>   but *you* will see me, ...

Then we have the reason:

> because *I live* and *you* will live.

Finally, we have the proclamation of the interrelationships that
now exist:

> On that day you will realize that *I* am in my *Father*
>   and *you* are in me and *I* in you.

Unstressed words need to be clearly heard but not given undue
emphasis. Listen, then, for the contrasts, the oppositions. These
help listeners to grasp the meaning easily.

d. *Intonation*

Intonation is the tune or melody that carries our words. All
languages have their own melody: French, German, Swedish,
Spanish, Russian. Chinese has many tones and depending which
one a speaker uses, the same word can have a different meaning.
Years ago two English voice teachers put together a handbook of
English intonation[24] based on the two tunes or melodies characteristic of the English language when spoken: the first is a falling
cadence on the stressed syllables that concludes with a firm
downward bend of the voice. If you were to notate this cadence
on paper, it would look like this. (Again, the stressed syllables
are marked with a dash, the unstressed with a dot.)

Thank you very much.

Take a phrase now from Scripture.

Jesus taught his disciples to pray.

The second melody is similar to the first: a descending series of stressed words but on the final syllable(s) there is an upward bend. The most common example of this is the simple phrase:

Once upon a time . . . .

Or try the biblical phrase:

Jesus said to his disciples, . . .

The rise at the end of the phrase on *time* and *disciples* allows for a number of possibilities. The most obvious is that it permits the speaker to pause so that listeners can absorb what has been said. A rising cadence can also indicate something more is coming, building anticipation in the listeners. Finally, a rise can imply that something is being left unsaid. Consider the rising cadence when asking this question:

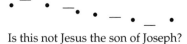

Is this not Jesus the son of Joseph?

Now try that same line with a simple descending cadence. What is the difference? The down cadence offers the statement as a simple question. But when one rises at the end of it, more is implied than a simple question requiring an answer of yes or no. One could imply surprise and wonder, saying the phrase with a tone of "Wow! I can't believe my eyes!" or one could imply more a reaction of "Who does he think he is?"

These two basic melodies allow for endless variations in vocal variety, depending on your ability to use your voice as an instrument. A sequence of sentences can be turned into an experience that moves listeners from fear to wonder. A difference in the starting note of the first stressed word allows for subtle shifts that can bring variety to speaking. Longer phrases can be handled in a way that the voice makes use of the falling cadence on stressed syllables but then goes back up at a certain point in a phrase to avoid "scraping bottom" before the end of the phrase. For instance, rather than descending on all five stressed syllables of the sentence below ("Master, . . . show . . . Father, . . . that . . . enough . . ."), your voice goes up again on "*that*":

"Master, show us the Father, and that will be enough for us."

The creativity comes in varying the use of the two melodies. Consider the following line from the words Jesus spoke in the Gospel of John on the night before he died.

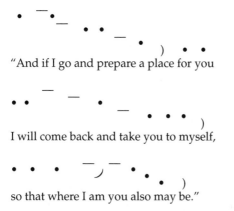

"And if I go and prepare a place for you

I will come back and take you to myself,

so that where I am you also may be."

Every reading invites a lector to create a musical score for it. As already mentioned, monotony comes from having a limited vocal repertoire of expression, being a Johnny/Janie-one-note or repeating the same vocal patterns over and over again. With subtle variations, based on sense and the emotional tenor of the texts, readings can be spoken in a fresh way.

e. *Diction*

Clear diction, articulation, enunciation—unless the words are said with good diction, all is lost. Saying the words clearly and precisely means spending enough time on the vowel sounds and making sure the consonants are given sufficient weight. If you are sloppy on the vowels, either too clipped or not making the appropriate sound (this is where any regional accent can be a problem), there will be no meaning conveyed because listeners do not understand you; if you are careless on the consonants, the result is gibberish and listeners do not understand you. Have you ever heard a lector conclude with something that sounded like: "The wer a the Lor" instead of "The wor*d* o*f* the Lor*d*"? Consider the difference when speaking clearly between p and b, t and d, f and v. The lips form the same way for each pair, but unless each is pronounced with care, we end up with "St. Ball the Aboslte" and "Touting Domas." M, n, l, v, dg (as in judge) require resonance in the body. On the other hand, there can be too much emphasis given. With *p* and *t* there is a danger of popping over the microphone; and *s* can hisss. Books with exercises in pronunciation can be helpful. Even experienced lectors might want to check on the state of their diction. The most immediate way is to ask a few people at Mass if they had any trouble understanding you.

f. *Pace*

The most frequent complaint? "That lector reads too fast." If you want to be understood, you cannot read as quickly as you talk in everyday conversation nor as you do on the telephone. First of all, the sound has to travel further in the church. Get in the habit of taking a few seconds before you begin a reading to look at the community. See who is furthest away from you—is there anyone up in the choir loft?—and read especially for that person. This awareness of the people furthest away will also affect your vocal range, the amount of emphasis you put on your words, your articulation—it all has to be "bigger." So, look out and about.

It is not the space alone that determines the pace. The content of the reading also will call for variation in your speed. When Jesus says, "Amen, Amen, I say to you . . . ," you know he is about to say something very important. A slower pace will give the statement greater weight. Sometimes a reading can be so short that if you don't slow down, it will not make any impression. Consider this optional reading from the book of Revelation for a funeral liturgy:

> I, John, heard a voice from heaven say, "Write this:
>   Blessed are the dead who die in the Lord from now on."
> "Yes," said the Spirit,
>   "let them find rest from their labors,
>   for their works accompany them."

That's it—two sentences! It is over before you know it. But notice there are three voices or speakers in these two sentences: the speaker (John), the voice from heaven, and the Spirit, so you can give this reading the power it deserves by careful pacing, allowing each voice to have its moment.

In contrast are those moments of dialogue when the pace can pick up, as in this exchange between Jesus and Peter at the Last Supper that is read on Holy Thursday:

> Peter said to him, "You will never wash my feet."
> Jesus answered him, "Unless I wash you, you will have no
>   inheritance with me."
> Simon Peter said to him, "Master, then not only my feet, but my
>   hands and head as well."

Familiarity can lead to reading too quickly. Some readers approach texts with the attitude that "we have all heard this so many times before" and they speed through the overly familiar text. But while we may have heard a text many times, this time it might speak to someone there for the first time. Remember, too, although you have spent time reading, studying, praying over and practicing the text, the listeners have not. For many, the last time they may have heard this reading could be three years ago, and if it was read poorly then or if a person was not paying attention, then six years might have gone by since this text got a hearing. So, approach every reading as if this were bring read for the first time; give yourself the time needed to absorb the thoughts and feelings, to see in your imagination the events happening in a story, to allow any questions asked in a text to hang in the air for a moment, to respond to the images the text sets out. Rushing through a reading is a very frustrating experience for a listener. And if the pace is at a breakneck speed, people will turn off.

On the other hand, it is possible to read too slowly. Then a reading becomes tedious, boring, and lifeless. But this is a relatively rare disease. Again, if you have any doubts one way or the other, ask if you are either a rapid-fire reader or a languid lector.

g. *Pausing*

Some people read like they drive, with as few stops along the way as possible. Others pause too often, causing listeners to lose the flow of thought. The present layout of the Lectionary is a great improvement from earlier editions where readers had to deal with paragraphs. With readings laid out in "sense lines," it is not only easier to see and not lose your place, but it gives a sense of where to pause. But this is not infallible. Just because the line stops does not necessarily mean you should. Put the words together that need to be linked in a "thought phrase," which can differ from a "sense line." A thought phrase holds the words together that need to be grouped according to the sense of what is being said. For instance, in this opening of the first reading from the prophet Jeremiah on the Sixteenth Sunday in Ordinary Time, Cycle B, you do not want to pause at the end of the first line but continue on:

> Woe to the shepherds
>> who mislead and scatter the flock of my pasture,
>> says the Lord.

Make the first two lines one "thought phrase" because it is "Woe to the shepherds-who-mislead-and-scatter-the-flock-of-my-pasture." If you pause after "shepherds," then the listener has to put the whole phrase together that spells out which particular shepherds are the subjects of Ezekiel's "woe." This same dynamic occurs in other readings when you have a relative clause, such as "the one who . . . ," "the Lord who . . . ," "God who. . ." The rest of the phrase completes the picture. And there need by only the slightest pause before saying, "says the Lord."

On the other hand, you might need some additional pausing in other "sense lines" to allow the important words to sink in. For instance, in the frequently read passage from the First Letter to the Corinthians, you have a series of pairings that describes love:

> Love is patient, love is kind.
> It is not jealous, it is not pompous,
>   it is not inflated, it is not rude,
>   it does not seek its own interests,
>   it is not quick-tempered, it does not brood over injury,
>   it does not rejoice over wrongdoing but rejoices with the truth.
> It bears all things, believes all things,
>   hopes all things, endures all things.
> Love never fails.

Give each one of love's attributes its due. Remember, in a long series like this, a rapid listing of one quality after another can have diminishing returns in listener comprehension. Take your time. Give each brush stroke in this portrait of love a careful application: "Love is patient, . . . kind, . . . not inflated, . . . not rude, . . . not seek its own interests, . . . not quick-tempered, . . . not brood over injury,"—but then you have an extended line with a contrast—". . . not rejoice over wrongdoing but rejoices over the truth." As a cherished teacher of mine used to say, "Always read it as if for the first time."

Finally, just as there needs to be variety in giving emphasis to words, some being stressed and others unstressed, so too in pausing. Some can be mere hesitations, enough for both reader and listener to catch a quick breath; others are more substantial, allowing a moment to think and ponder what has just been said. Always pause when people are first sitting down after the opening prayer to listen to the word. Let them get settled. Wait for the rustling and movement to stop. This gives you a chance to look at your listeners, to make initial contact with them before speaking. Then, after announcing where the text is from, pause again. Most importantly, at the conclusion of the reading, allow for a good pause before announcing, "The word of the Lord." I would suggest counting quietly: "1001, 1002, 1003," then say,

"The word of the Lord." Otherwise, this phrase sounds like it is part of the reading, rather than a proclamation of faith calling for a response from the community. And remember, as many times as you say them, appreciate the importance of these words: the faith of the lector is calling to the faith of the community: "The word of the Lord." "Thanks be to God."

h. *Eye Contact*

A frequent word of advice for public speakers is to have eye contact with their audience. This also holds for lectors but there are some nuances to keep in mind. Years ago I heard the expression "person contact" instead of eye contact. You want to make listeners feel you are reading to them, which involves now and then a moment of genuine connection with listeners, not a darting glance from a head bobbing up and down, nor a sweeping eye/windshield wiper movement across the church that really looks at no one, nor a look over the heads of listeners. Watch for falling into a mechanical pattern: up and to the right, up and to the left, right, left. Take the time to look, but not glare, at various people sitting in the different sections of the church—and don't forget the choir loft.

There are times when making eye contact is appropriate, for instance, at the opening announcement of the reading, and at the end when making the proclamation of faith: "The word of the Lord." Also, when you are reading the responsorial psalm and want to bring people in for their response, bring them in with your eyes, by looking up. I have seen lectors resort to some overt gesture at this time, even pushing an arm straight out in a dramatic flourish, as an indication of when to respond. At best the gesture is unnecessary, at worse, awkward and stiff. Use your voice (slow down and use a strong final cadence) and eyes (look up) to bring people in at the end of each verse.

During the reading, you might want to make eye contact at certain points but not at others. The former occasions are fairly obvious: when the words of the text are as much for our salvation as for anyone else's. Such an instance would be Paul's words to the Thessalonians: "Rejoice always. Pray without ceasing," or when a narrator is imparting information, especially at the beginning or end of a story. But when a character is speaking to another in a story, you might want to place the character spoken to above the heads of your listeners so they do not think these words are aimed at them. This can be true even when Jesus is speaking, especially if he is chastising the Pharisees or annoyed with the apostles. You probably do not want to be looking at anyone when John the Baptist is calling the Pharisees a brood of vipers or Paul is calling the Galatians stupid.

i. *Making Mistakes*

We do make mistakes on occasion, even after preparing. Is it better to keep moving on or go back and read it correctly? Announcing Paul's Letter to the Philippines or even reading "Then Jesus went out and hung himself" during the Passion might be better off left behind as quickly as possible, leaving listeners to make the obvious correction. However, if there is a *serious* change in the meaning of a statement that either contradicts the text's meaning or could baffle or confuse the community, it is best to go back and re-read what has been misread. The lector who read, ". . . that which is mortal must clothe itself with *immorality*" rather than ". . . with *immortality*" was correct to go back and re-read the sentence. Don't get flustered; a slight pause followed by an "Excuse me," then a re-reading, is sufficient. Watch, though, that you do not re-read too quickly, as there is a tendency to do, assuming people already heard most of the phrase or sentence except for the mistake. Give the thought its full value; read it as if for the first time, which, indeed, it is.

The requirements of the listener are as important as the requirements of the word of God itself. You can have a deep and profound understanding of the particular text you are appointed to read, but if people cannot hear you (more possible than ever today with an increasing number of people experiencing hearing difficulties sooner rather than later), if people can't distinguish what you are saying because of the quality of your voice, or a heavy accent, or because you mumble, slur, or mispronounce words, or because your pace is either too frantic or lethargic—then all your understanding and love for the Scriptures will not carry over in bringing it to others. It can be humbling to ask another person, "Can you understand me when I am reading? Is there anything you think would improve my reading of the Scriptures?" But the role of lector is a ministry, and being a good servant in this area means realizing that there is usually always room for further growth and improvement.

KEEP IN MIND

A checklist of reading requirements that benefit the listeners:

- Voice Quality: a clear, natural, full voice.

- Vocal Variety: a range of voice that avoids monotony and singsong or overly repetitious vocal patterns.

- Rhythm: recognizing what words are to be stressed and unstressed; certain poetic forms are given a rhythm of three or four beats per line.

- Intonation: there are two basic tunes or melodies that carry our words and help bring variety to public reading.

- Diction: clear articulation of consonants and enunciation of vowels.

- Pace: provide variety in speed but neither too slow nor too fast.

- Pause: Allowing time for listeners to comprehend what has been said.

- Person-contact rather than eye contact when appropriate to the text.

- Correct your mistakes when necessary to dispel confusion or misunderstanding.

The requirements of the setting. A final area that influences the reading of the word of God is the setting. It is obvious that readers experience different demands when they lector in a large cathedral or a small chapel, have a good microphone or a poor one, are reading to a diverse community on Sunday, at a school Mass for young children, or at a residence for seniors where some in attendance may have hearing problems. The setting brings its own demands. By "setting" I also would include the liturgical setting: whether a Mass, another sacramental celebration, or a special occasion during which the word of God is read.

a. *Energy*

Energy is a relative factor, both in personality and in what is needed to do a task. People by nature have different energy levels. When it comes to lectoring, the energy level needed is determined by a combination of factors. The selection itself can demand a certain amount of energy; compare Luke's account of Pentecost in Acts with the gospel for Pentecost Sunday from John. Different energy levels are needed. And certain occasions seem to call for higher energy simply because of the community present, for instance, the Children's or Family Mass. Space also determines the amount of energy needed. Some lectors have a very intimate reading style that does well in a small setting but comes off as low-energy after the first few benches of a large space. Then there is a need to crank up the wattage. Practice with the space in mind.

Energy level influences how involved you are and are perceived to be in what you are doing. As already mentioned, it is not enough to have only your voice engaged. A full reading involves your face, body, mind, feelings, and imagination. You might even use a mirror to see if your face is registering what the words are saying. Does your face communicate the proclamation: "Rejoice in the Lord always. I shall say it again: rejoice." I am not suggesting grinning from ear to ear, but does your face mirror your words? Engagement of the whole person involves walking the line between low-keyed and lifeless on the one side, and exaggerated and excessive on the other.

Allow the body to participate. In the study of body movement, there is a difference captured in the words *kinesics* and *kinesthesis*. The former concerns the study of body movement in relation to speaking and deals with the overt, physical gestures we make when we speak: for instance putting out an arm and yelling, "STOP!" Here, you experience your body in action.

Kinesthesis, however, concerns the sensation of body movement, position, and muscular tension. "Kinesthetic activity is as vital an aspect of reading as it is of daily living."[25] An example might be to imagine you are scraping your fingernail on a blackboard. What do you feel in your body? You might find it helpful to use physical gestures when you practice a reading, even though you will not do this during the public proclamation of the word. The body, however, remembers the gesture and responds, leading to a greater physical engagement during the reading.

b. *Microphones*

Make friends with your mike. First, make sure it is pointed toward your mouth and not still adjusted for the person before you. Microphones differ. Some are unidirectional, meaning you have to read directly into them; others are omni-directional, so you can move your head, turn to the right and the left, and the microphone will pick up the sound. Mikes also vary in quality, some being very sensitive, some tinny, some needing great care with diction, while others will need you to be careful with some of the more explosive sounds like p's and t's. Most importantly, remember that the microphone will not do all the work. Using a microphone does not mean you can read in your normal tone of voice and that will be enough. Mikes are not magic, transforming a feeble sound into what is loud, clear, and intelligible. Think of the mike as a collaborator, helping to amplify what you present with sufficient energy.

c. *Nervousness*

"Will I ever get over being nervous?" is a question beginners often ask. Probably. But that might not be a good thing. A little nervousness can be helpful, keeping us attentive and engaged. The adrenalin is up because you are aware of the importance of what you are doing. You are proclaiming the word of God and a reverential case of "nerves" is not out of place. Often nervousness will fade the more you lector, get used to being up before the community, and grow in confidence in your ability to lector well.

In the face of extreme nervousness, you might ask: What is making me so nervous? Where is the focus? Am I worried about what other people are thinking, how they will evaluate me? Will they like me? Here is where concentration can be helpful. I remember Katharine Hepburn appearing on the Dick Cavett Show years ago. Referring to Spencer Tracey and why he was such a great actor, she said, "It was concentration, concentration, concentration. His concentration was pure. He would be talking to you one moment, then the cameras would go on and he would be in character. A great gift for concentration." Then, she said, "I have found that if the material was wonderful . . . and if I could really and truly concentrate and if I could really speak English and with truth—mind's truth and heart's truth—hand a scene to an audience, and if they were concentrating, they would just take it. If it has heart's truth so that it strikes right through, you can say, 'Oh, I understand what you mean.'" Use concentration on the text as a shield against nervousness. Move your focus away from yourself.

Before reading, certain exercises can help you relax, for example, breathing slowly, from the diaphragm. Place your hand on your stomach—it should expand when you inhale and contract when you exhale. Some people sing scales or play with nonsense sounds as mentioned earlier, using a wide vocal range. And, of course, there is prayer. Place yourself in the presence of God who has called you to speak the living Word to God's own people. Ask the Holy Spirit to fill your heart and enlighten your mind, to give you courage and inner peace.

d. *Familiarity with the Reading*

Another way to combat nervousness is by being familiar with the reading. Read it aloud throughout the week before you lector. Becoming comfortable with the phrasing, the shifts in emotion or the turns in the storyline, and making decisions about where to pause and when to look up, brings not only a level of confidence but allows you the freedom to look away from the text without fear of losing your place. Some readers and presiders memorize the text and present it as a memorized piece. This can come off as showy, and I wonder if listeners find themselves more caught up watching whether the reader will get through it without going blank than in being attentive to the word being spoken. It is "A reading from . . . ," not "A performance of . . . ." Still, if a good memory is a gift you have been blessed with, memorizing a selection can help to make a selection your own, while still presenting it to the community as a reading

e. *The Language of Liturgy*

In his *Guide For Lectors*, Aelred Rosser, O.S.B., comments that "ritual language is more formative than informative, concerned more with 'doing' than with 'telling.'"[26] Such language acts on us in profound ways, forming not only our attitudes and values but providing the dominant images of God, the People of God, and the individual as a child of God in Christ. When one constantly hears the masculine pronoun in the biblical texts, whether applied to God or to humans, this inevitably has an effect on those listening, shaping how we "see" God and making us feel included or excluded as recipients of the word of God.

An ongoing issue, especially in light of the most recent revision of the Roman Catholic *Lectionary for Mass*, is whether lectors can change any of the language in the lectionary text to make it more inclusive; for instance, changing "he" to "you" or "they" or some other formulation that would include both men and women. One can only wonder why the decision was made to continue to use exclusive language when another choice was possible, as exemplified by the New Revised Standard Version of the Bible. As a matter of fact, the present translation of the Psalms in the *Lectionary for Mass* is frequently more exclusive than that found in the 1969 Lectionary. Lectors and proclaimers of the gospel are presented with texts such as:

> Before *man* are life and death, good and evil,
>> Whichever *he* chooses shall be given *him*.
> (Sirach, Sixth Sunday in Ordinary Time, Cycle A)

> Blessed the *man* who follows not
>> the counsel of the wicked, . . .
> (Responsorial Psalm, Sixth Sunday in Ordinary Time, Cycle C)

Therefore, whoever thinks *he* is standing secure
    should take care not to fall.
    (1 Corinthians Third Sunday of Lent, Cycle C)

Come after me, and I will make you fishers of *men*.
    (Gospel of Mark, Third Sunday in Ordinary Time, Cycle B)

And whoever loves me will be loved by my Father
    and I will love *him* and reveal myself to *him*.
        (Gospel of John, Sixth Sunday of Easter, Cycle A)

And on and on it goes throughout the Lectionary. While it would be irresponsible to encourage a lector freely to change such texts, one can only hope that a further revision will address this issue in the near future. In the meantime, care should be taken to consult diocesan liturgical offices to see if there are any recommendations in place to deal with the issue of liturgical and biblical language that needlessly excludes more than half of those in attendance. The liturgy of the community should reflect the wisdom of the community.

f. *Dress and Ornamentation*

Dress should be appropriate to the setting. The *General Instruction of the Roman Missal* observes: "In the dioceses of the United States of America, acolytes, altar servers, lectors, and other lay ministers may wear the alb or other suitable vesture or other appropriate and dignified clothing" (339). Nothing should distract or call attention to you, either by its inappropriateness or its costliness. Unless you are reading at the parish picnic, your dress should be determined by an awareness that this is a sacred space and you are engaged in a sacred action. Neither beachwear, playground togs, nor cocktail party ensembles will do. Try not to be a billboard for Nike or a promotion for whatever team can claim you as a fan. Avoid sweatshirts, T-shirts, and anything with a slogan. The only word listeners should focus on is God's word. And you should neither glitter nor sparkle. Save the jewelry—even watches and tie clips—for the next gala. A quick rule of thumb regarding jewelry and clothing is: take off the former and put on the latter—not vice versa! You are reading the word of God to the people of God.

g. *The Symbols at Hand*

Liturgy is rich in symbols. The primary symbols in the Liturgy of the Word are the books that contain the readings and the ambo where the readings occur. "The readings are always to be proclaimed at the ambo" (LMIn, 16). This ambo should be "somewhat elevated, fixed, and of a suitable design and nobility" (32). It is reserved for the readings, the responsorial psalm, the homily, and the prayer of the faithful; in addition, the Exsultet is sung from here at the Easter Vigil. Since the ambo serves as the table of the word, it is worthy of reverence. Your manner of approaching it should reflect that you are drawing near to holy ground.

The books that contain the readings "remind the hearers of the presence of God speaking to his people. Since they serve as signs and symbols of the higher realities, care must be taken to ensure that they truly are worthy, dignified and beautiful" (33). The lector has a special relationship to these books; they should not be treated as props but handled with the high regard they deserve as the signs of God's presence with us in the word. The Lectionary should always be used for reading, never a missalette or binder—the equivalent of using a paper plate and a Styrofoam cup for the Eucharist. The *Book of the Gospels* receives special honor by being carried up in the procession with great reverence and placed on the altar; it will be carried over to the ambo at the time of the reading of the gospel. Incense may also be used as an expression of our reverence for the word of God that it contains. But be careful when replacing the *Lectionary for Mass* with the *Book of the Gospels* that the former is treated with respect and honor. It should be clear who takes the Lectionary and where it is to be placed.

h. *Early Arrival on the Scene*

A final recommendation is to arrive early, at least fifteen minutes before the liturgy begins. Check on the book to make sure it is set up correctly, with the ribbons in the proper place. Trying to find the reading when the marker has been moved or has slipped out can be an experience when not only time seems to stand still but also one's ability to locate the proper place.

Furthermore, there are those solemnities, feasts, and special occasions when the Lectionary offers various options (for instance, the second reading on Easter and Pentecost or the readings on certain feasts of the saints or on the occasion of an anointing). Unless this has been clarified beforehand, you might find yourself facing a reading you have not practiced.

KEEP IN MIND

Like the text and the listeners, the setting places its own demand on the lector. Some of the factors to keep in mind are:

- Keep your energy level appropriate to the space where you are reading.
- Make friends with the microphone; think of it as a collaborator.
- Nervousness is not always bad; use concentration as a protection against excessive anxiety.
- Familiarity with the reading can help to make you comfortable with your surroundings.
- The language of the translation can be problematic; keep aware of any developments in this regard.
- Clothing and jewelry can distract; help listeners attend to the word.
- Both ambo and the books are signs of God's presence and deserving of our reverence.
- An early arrival in the sacristy can help forestall getting lost in the Lectionary.

From Skill to Art: Four Suggestions

We all tend to reach plateaus in any human endeavor in which we engage. This is especially true for any performance skill: dancing, singing, acting, playing an instrument—and lectoring. A skill progresses into an art over time. Four suggestions to this end:

a. Finding feedback and support in your ministry. Practice does not necessarily make perfect; sometimes it only makes permanent. Ask for feedback. Family and friends can often make good suggestions, if you let them know you are open to hearing from them. But a helpful suggestion here: Don't ask and then argue with the response. Just say "thank you" and think about what the other person has said. Asking another lector can be particularly helpful, especially one who has achieved a high level of performance. Getting together occasionally with the other lectors appointed for the same Sunday to pray over, discuss, and practice before the Sunday liturgy can provide opportunity for obtaining feedback and also provide a deeper sense of community with those who share this ministry. Another possibility would be to have periodic viewings of readings that are videotaped during the liturgy itself.

b. Attending workshops. Lector workshops should be a regular occurrence. They can especially help you to prepare for the coming liturgical seasons: Advent-Christmas, Lent-Easter, and Ordinary Time. A workshop before each season can provide input on the upcoming readings, and possibly a videotaping of certain ones. There is no substitute for using a camcorder to see what you are and are not doing. A person can be told something many times, but frequently not until it is seen on the video does it become fully conscious. "I am reading much faster than I thought," is one of the most frequent reactions; along with, "I thought I was putting much more life into that."

c. Listen to good readers. Over the past year I have listened to some wonderful books on tape. Jim Dale's reading of J. K. Rowling's *Harry Potter* series is a marvel; in the latest book, he creates more than 130 characters. Although I do not encourage putting on voices when reading Scripture as he does here, still, listen for vocal variety, range, pace, rhythm, and so many of the qualities essential to good reading. Ed Herrmann's reading of the award-winning historical study *John Adams* by David McCullough was also a treat. And, most recently, actress Joan Allen was nominated for an audio award for her reading of Carol Shield's novel *Unless.*

d. Become a lover of the Scriptures. Most importantly, come to know intimately the book you are called to read. Spend time not only with the Lectionary but also with the Bible. Fr. Gerard

Sloyan writes: "The qualified lector is a person who often reads the Bible privately. His or her intimate knowledge of it and enthusiasm for it is infectious."[27] Try to read the complete books of the Bible, not just a snippet here and there. God has called you to be the instrument through which God's word comes alive. So, dwell with the word of God. Find a home in it. Pray with and through it. To grow in understanding there are numerous commentaries that are both helpful and exciting to read. Some resources for further reading are at the end of this book.

A Final Word

"People read to know they're not alone."

The word of God proclaimed when the community of believers gathers to worship brings this thought to fulfillment in a most profound way. When the word of God is read, we come to know we are not alone. The word of God mediates presence, human and divine. It acts to bring its hearers into communion, linking all who listen at this moment with one another, with those known and unknown authors whose words continue to be read aloud year after year, and with all those who form that great throng of believers who over countless generations have heard these words in their own day and have been nourished and sustained by them. But, most of all, these words entrusted now to us, bind us anew to the One who is the origin of these words, who has spoken "in times past in partial and various ways," but who in the fullness of time spoke to us through the Son "whom he made heir of all things and through whom he created the universe, who is the refulgence of his glory, the very imprint of his being, and who sustains all things by his mighty word" (Heb 1:1-3a). When we hear God's word and accept it in faith, truly we are not alone.

As lectors, then, we are given the improbable task of expressing the inexpressible: God's unfathomable and ongoing love for all creation, God's ongoing plan of redemption and salvation for all the world, God's ongoing work of sanctifying all who have been made in the divine image. From the beginning God has called others to help bring this work to completion, and God continues to enlist the efforts of all the children of the various faith traditions, but especially those who have been adopted as sons and daughters through water and the Spirit, and who gather to break the bread and share the cup of the crucified and risen Lord Jesus Christ. In order for this great act of worship to be done with faith, women and men are appointed to this ministry of lector, joining that long line of prophets—Moses and Miriam, Isaiah and Hulda, Jeremiah, Ezekiel, Daniel, Anna and Simeon, Mary of Nazareth, Peter and Paul, the beloved disciple and Mary Magdalene—through whom the word of the Lord has been spoken to the people God chose as peculiarly God's own. The fulfillment of this ministry currently rests with us. And so, my friends: "Let the word of God dwell in you richly . . ." (Col 3: 16).

The *Book of Blessings* provides an order of blessing of readers that can be done within Mass. It is distinct from the institution of readers by the bishop. This blessing is for parish readers who have the responsibility to proclaim the Scriptures at Mass and other liturgical services and is to be given by the pastor or his delegate. It follows the Liturgy of the Word. I will conclude this work with this prayer of blessing.

> Everlasting God,
> when he read in the synagogue at Nazareth,
> your Son proclaimed the good news of salvation
> for which he would give up his life.
>
> Bless these readers.
> As they proclaim your words of life,
> strengthen their faith
> that they may read with conviction and boldness,
> and put into practice what they read.
> We ask this through Christ our Lord.
> Amen.

Notes

[1] *General Instruction of the Roman Missal* (Third Typical Edition) Washington, D.C.: United States Conference of Catholic Bishops, 2003.

[2] All quotations from the documents of the Second Vatican Council are taken from *The Basic Sixteen Documents, Vatican Council II: Constitutions, Decrees, Declarations. A Completely Revised Translation in Inclusive Language*, ed. Austin Flannery, O.P. (Northport, N.Y.: Costello Publishing Co., 1996).

[3] Ann Sexton, "Words," *The Awful Rowing Towards God* (Boston: Houghton Mifflin, 1975) 71.

[4] Tom Stoppard, *The Real Thing* (London: Faber and Faber, 1983) 54.

[5] Justin Martyr, The First Apology, ch. 67, *Writings of St. Justin Martyr*, trans. Thomas B. Falls (New York: Christian Heritage, 1948) 106–7.

[6] Perry H. Biddle, Jr., "Preaching the Lectionary," in *The New Dictionary of Sacramental Worship*, ed. Peter E. Fink, S.J. (Collegeville: Liturgical Press, 1990) 979.

[7] Quoted by Kate Dooley in *To Listen and Tell: Introduction to the Lectionary for Masses with Children. With Commentary by Kate Dooley* (Washington, D.C.: Pastoral Press, 1993) 31.

[8] Martin Connell, *Guide to the Revised Lectionary* (Chicago: Liturgy Training Publications, 1998) 5.

[9] Ibid., 12–13.

[10] Dooley, 22. See this excellent commentary for further insights into the rationale and intention of the *Lectionary for Masses with Children*.

[11] Don Oldenburg, "Now Hear This & Pay Attention!" *The Washington Post* (February 20, 2001) C4.

[12] St. Augustine, *The Confessions of St. Augustine, Books I–X*, trans F. J. Sheed (New York: Sheed and Ward, 1942) 89.

[13] Michael Downey, *Trappist: Living in the Land of Desire* (New York: Paulist, 1997) 90.

[14] John J. Pilch, *The Cultural Dictionary of the Bible* (Collegeville: Liturgical Press, 1999) 22–23. Pilch has also written books on each of the Sunday readings in the three cycles: *The Cultural World of the Gospels*, *The Cultural World of the Apostles*, and *The Cultural World of the Prophets*. All are published by the Liturgical Press, Collegeville, Minnesota.

[15] Pilch, *Cultural Dictionary*, 2–3.

[16] Dianne Bergant, with Richard Fragomeni, *Preaching the New Lectionary, Year B* (Collegeville: The Liturgical Press, 1999) 214–15. This is a three-volume series for the three-year Sunday cycle: A, B, and C.

[17] Charlotte Lee, *Oral Interpretation*, 4th ed. (Boston: Houghton Mifflin Co., 1971) 2.

[18] Wallace Bacon, *The Art of Interpretation* (New York: Holt, Rinehart, and Winston, 1972) 232–39.

[19] Ibid., 34.

[20] Alla Bozarth-Campbell, *The Word's Body: An Incarnational Aesthetic of Interpretation* (Tuscaloosa, Ala.: University of Alabama Press, 1979) 20.

[21] Walter Brueggemann, *Genesis* (Atlanta: John Knox Press, 1982) 40–54.

[22] Sloyan, 122.

[23] Rabbi Herbert Bronstein, Helen Cahill, O.P., and Syafa'atun Elmirzana, "Prayer in the Abrahamic Faiths," *New Theology Review* (August, 2003) 23.

[24] Lilias E. Armstrong, and Ida C. Ward, *A Handbook of English Intonation* (Cambridge: W. Heffer & Sons, 1963).

[25] Bacon, 11.

[26] Aelred Rosser, O.S.B., *Guide For Lectors* (Chicago: Liturgy Training Publications, 1998) 37.

[27] Sloyan, 119.

Resources

A. For Deeper Understanding of the Scripture Readings

Bergant, Dianne, with Richard Fragomeni. *Preaching the New Lectionary, Year A, B, C*. Collegeville: Liturgical Press, 1999, 2000, 2001.

These three volumes offer commentary on the readings for Sunday and the major feasts of the particular year (A, B, C), identify the various themes that link the readings, and provide overviews of the liturgical seasons and the relationship of the readings across a period of time.

The Collegeville Bible Commentery (based on the New American Bible with revised New Testament). Gen. eds. Dianne Bergant, Robert J. Karris. Collegeville: Liturgical Press, 1989.

A reference work with the latest in biblical scholarship: literary, historical, and theological.

Collegeville Pastoral Dictionary of Biblical Theology. Collegeville: Liturgical Press, 1996.

This work with more than 500 entries provides lectors the opportunity for deepening their understanding of the Bible.

Days of the Lord, The Liturgical Year. 7 vols. Collegeville: Liturgical Press, 1991–1994.

A seven-volume series that contains commentary on all the Sunday readings and all major feasts.

Pilch, John. *The Cultural Dictionary of the Bible*. Collegeville: Liturgical Press, 1999. Also of interest are *The Cultural World of the Gospels, A, B, C; The Cultural World of the Apostles, A, B, C;* and *The Cultural World of the Prophets, A, B, C.*

John Pilch's various works offer an understanding and appreciation for the cultural customs, attitudes, and values that underlie the biblical world.

B. For Assistance in Proclaiming the Readings

Staubacher, Joseph M. *Lector's Guide to Biblical Pronunciation, Updated.* Huntington, Ind.: Our Sunday Visitor Publishing Division, 2001.

A helpful book providing not only an alphabetized listing of names, places, and things that give a lector pause but also a Sunday by Sunday guide.

Workbook for Lectors and Gospel Readers. Chicago: Liturgy Training Publications, annual.

An annual resource that offers brief commentary, markings, and suggestions regarding emphasis and pausing for all the Sunday readings.

Zimmermann, Joyce Ann, Thomas A. Greisen, Kathleen Harmon, S.N.D.de N., and Thomas L. Leclerc, M.S., *Living Light: Spirituality, Celebration, and Catechesis for Sundays and Solemnities.* Collegeville: Liturgical Press, annual.

Designed to bring life and liturgy together, this team effort gives lectors valuable assistance in their spiritual preparation.

C. For a Deeper Appreciation of the Liturgy of the Word

Power, David N. *The Word of the Lord, Liturgy's Use of Scripture.* Maryknoll, N.Y.: Orbis, 2001.

A short work "for all who struggle to interpret the Word responsibly" by one of the noted liturgical theologians of our day to assist lectors in appreciating how Scripture texts help listeners hear the Gospel of Christ.

West, Fritz. *Scripture and Memory, The Ecumenical Hermeneutic of the Three-Year Lectionary.* Collegeville: Liturgical Press, 1997.

A study of the three year lectionaries used by both Catholic and Protestant churches as a result of the Second Vatican Council's mandate to offer a richer selection of biblical texts for worship. The author highlights the important differences between the Roman Catholic *Lectionary for Mass* and the *Revised Common Lectionary* used by many of the Protestant churches.